Do Sourdough

Slow Bread for Busy Lives

Andrew Whitley

Published by
The Do Book Company 2014
Works in Progress Publishing Ltd
thedobook.co

A CIP catalogue record for this book
is available from the British Library

ISBN 978-1-907974-11-3

11

To find out more about our company,
books and authors, please visit
thedobook.co or follow us **@dobookco**

5% of our proceeds from the sale of
this book is given to The Do Lectures
to help it achieve its aim of making
positive change **thedolectures.com**

Cover designed by James Victore
Book designed and set by Ratiotype

This edition printed and bound
by OZGraf Print on Munken,
an FSC® certified paper

MIX
Paper from
responsible sources
FSC
www.fsc.org   FSC® C163799

Contents

Simple sourdough wheat bread

1
What Is Sourdough?

Sourdough bread is all the rage. It takes pride of place in every artisan or micro-bakery. It has helped countless people enjoy bread again after years of digestive discomfort associated with speedily produced industrial loaves. It even appears in supermarkets.
A product has well and truly emerged from its niche when it has been adopted by multiple retailers. However, their habitual tendency to dumb down and cut corners has, predictably enough, spawned loaves that are sourdough more by name than nature. As a result, many people's first taste of sourdough is both disappointing and inauthentic. One sure way to avoid this experience is to bake bread at home, as more and more people are doing.

Yet while many of us feel an urge to try sourdough, we can't imagine ever having the time (or skill) to master it.

Until now.

This book has two purposes: to dispel the myths that make sourdough seem complicated and intimidating; and to show how slow fermentation, with all its benefits, is both easy to manage and ideally suited to today's busy lifestyles.

Everyone – in fact, anyone – can DO sourdough. Here's why (and how).

Sourdough is ...

... just flour and water. It's that simple.

Given time and a little warmth, the yeasts and beneficial bacteria that are naturally present in the flour begin to multiply. The yeasts produce the carbon dioxide gas that makes the bread rise. The bacteria bring flavour and make the bread more nutritious and digestible.

Sourdough is economical. No need to seek out fresh yeast or pay extra for 'fast-acting' dried yeast (and its questionable additives). Just make a 'starter' with flour and water. Once this is fermenting well it can be used to make breads of all kinds – wholemeal, white, savoury and sweet.

The sourdough process is easy to manage. Refresh the starter with flour and water, let it ferment for a while, then use most of this to make bread, keeping a little back for the next batch – and so on, for ever.

Time is of the essence

The best breads are fermented slowly, which is exactly how sourdough yeasts and bacteria work. But they can do this while you, the baker, are asleep, at work or otherwise enjoying yourself. The slower a dough is rising, the longer the 'window' for getting it into the oven in good shape. You can bake to your own timetable, not one imposed by impatient yeast. Not much of your time is involved, unless you want it to be.

What's more, slow bread keeps better, lasts longer and is more satisfying. Quick loaves, puffed up with instant yeast, soon dry out and crumble. All too often, their fermentative legacy lingers on in the form of bloating and bowel trouble.

Above all, sourdough is fun. While it's easy to get good results simply by following the instructions, few people

Russian sourdough rye bread

fail to be fascinated by the 'miracle' of flour and water coming to life. Working with natural processes seems to spark a spirit of enquiry and experimentation. The more we learn, the more conscious we become of the profound beauty of what we see. Sourdough bread-making is a craft that produces not only nourishing daily bread but reasons a-plenty to keep having another go.

Keeping it simple

Baking with sourdough is so easy that it would be a pity if anyone were put off by the misinformation and tendency to overcomplicate that bedevil some of the advice on offer. So, take heart. You may safely ignore any methods or recipes that demand hours of kitchen time, use arcane vocabulary and make you take yourself just a little too seriously. Such methods are usually based on a poor grasp of the underlying biology, both human and microbial. It's useful before we begin to bear in mind the following:

— **A sourdough starter is made from nothing more than flour and water.** Adding apples, oranges, grapes, raisins, yoghurt, rhubarb or other presumed sources of useful microbes is unnecessary and a waste of time and money. These ingredients harbour strains of yeasts and bacteria that are, in the main, symbiotic with them and not with wheat or rye. They may not do any harm in your starter, but they are, at best, irrelevant.

— **Sourdoughs don't need regular 'feeding'.** They are not like pets or children, requiring three square meals a day to thrive. Unlike mammals, micro-organisms such as yeasts and bacteria do not die when they run short of food. They slow down, naturally, and in some cases produce spores that can survive for years – rather like weed seeds buried in undisturbed soil. A sourdough starter of mine was still viable after five years in the fridge with no additional nourishment of any kind. What sourdough starters do need, when you want to make bread with them, is refreshing. And we'll come to that shortly. For now you should certainly give a wide berth to any instructions that tell you to throw away excess starter, an excess caused entirely by unnecessary 'feeds'. This book promises not to waste your money or precious food.

Long time passing

Before yeast was identified and commercialised, ordinary people fed themselves with what we now call 'sourdough' bread and did so without the benefits of literacy, numeracy or celebrity chefs. So it really shouldn't be beyond us now.

Our forebears relied on the yeasts naturally present in the flour to make their bread rise. This took a long time, during which the bacteria that are also there could work their modest miracles – of flavour, nourishment and digestibility.

With the introduction of manufactured yeast in the 19th century things changed fundamentally. Isolated cultures of baker's yeast, usually strains of *Saccharomyces cerevisiae*, were chosen for their ability to produce masses of carbon dioxide quickly. This yeast was grown, not as part of the bread-making process, but quite separately, in large fermenters fed with a 'substrate' of coarse unrefined sugar known as molasses. The end product was either liquid, 'compressed' (fresh) or dried yeast, all of them very concentrated. There are roughly 30 billion yeast cells in one gram of fresh yeast – many orders of magnitude more than in even a well-developed sourdough starter.

With yeast available in such a concentrated form, it became possible to get dough to rise quickly, which meant there was much less opportunity for any beneficial bacteria to develop. However, 'German' yeast, as it was often known in 19th-century Britain, was expensive. So bakers would eke it out by using a two-stage process, known as 'sponge-and-dough'. A sponge was made with between a quarter and a half of the total requirement of flour and water in the recipe plus a small amount of yeast. Overnight, the yeast in the sponge would multiply. It takes a yeast cell a couple of hours to reproduce itself, so that over the 16 hours of a typical overnight sponge, this process could happen several times, resulting in a massive increase in the yeast population. When the sponge was added to the remaining flour and water (plus salt, fat, etc.) to make the main dough, there would be enough yeast cells to make the loaves rise in two or three hours.

With the 'sponge' method (also known as *poolish* in French and *biga* in Italian), there is time for some bacterial fermentation to take place, though not nearly as much as in a sourdough that is made without added yeast. This is why bread made with yeast in an overnight sponge-and-dough system has better flavour and keeping quality than bread made quickly in a 'straight' process, where all the ingredients are mixed in one go.

Yet, despite its qualities, sponge-and-dough (in Britain at least) fell victim to the age-old industrial imperative – to take time and skill out of the process. Yeast became cheaper, chemical 'improvers' were developed and high-speed mixing whipped up a loaf needing no 'bulk' fermentation time at all. 'No time' bread was cheap, to be sure. But the bread-eating public had been robbed of all the benefits that come with the slow maturation of dough – benefits that only 'real' sourdough brings.

What a difference a dough makes

Real sourdough? You mean not all sourdoughs are created equal? Sadly, no. But this doesn't make doing sourdough any more difficult. In fact, proper sourdough is the simplest there is, and the best. Which is why it's good to be able to recognise the impostors.

There is currently no legal definition of sourdough in the UK. As a result, 'sourdough' breads are popping up in the unlikeliest of places, including in what Chris Young of the Real Bread Campaign refers to as the 'loaf-tanning salons' that started life as in-store 'bakeries'. Often, these loaves are half-baked elsewhere, frozen and then given a 'bake tan' in a hot oven near the point of sale. In some cases, they are fully baked elsewhere and simply put out for sale near the in-store bakery as if to imply that they've been freshly made on the premises. The process is often reduced to 'baking by numbers', where the only skill required is to open the correct sachet of chemicals and enzymes and press the right buttons to set in train a semi-automated process of mixing, moulding and baking where human intervention is kept to a minimum.

So how do they come to be selling 'sourdough' loaves – or *pseudough*, as I prefer to think of them? Simple. They add a little 'dried sourdough' into a yeasted dough recipe. It rises in about the same time as an ordinary bread (i.e. very quickly) and may have just enough flavour to leave you wondering if it is really supposed to be there. That's it. No fresh, live sourdough starter. No time for any sourdough bacteria to make a difference. Just a little bit of powder from the chemistry set, lots of yeast as usual – and that'll be £1.75, thank you very much.

Added yeast has no place in real sourdough because in speeding up the rising it limits the multiple benefits that occur *only* when beneficial bacteria have time enough to work. Here's a short list of some of the health benefits of making bread harnessing the lactic acid bacteria (LAB) that are the key microbes in a typical sourdough:

— Sourdough LAB can neutralise the bits of gliadin and glutenin protein in wheat flour that are toxic to people with coeliac disease (CD) and non-coeliac gluten sensitivity. This doesn't mean CD sufferers can eat all (or even any) sourdough bread. It *does* mean that there is a time-honoured method for making wheat flour more digestible and that we urgently need to know which types of bread on sale in the shops deploy this to real effect.

— LAB (including those commonly found in sourdough bread) produce beneficial compounds: antioxidants, the cancer-preventive peptide lunasin, and anti-allergenic substances, some of which may help in the treatment of auto-immune diseases. These by-products seem able to survive the heat of baking, suggesting that sourdough bread could stimulate immune responses in the gut.

— Several hours of fermentation with sourdough is sufficient to neutralise the phytic acid that commonly 'locks up' minerals such as iron, calcium, magnesium and zinc in fast-fermented wholemeal breads.

— Bread is often avoided by those affected by weight-gain and metabolic syndrome – rightly, perhaps, in the case of industrial white loaves with a high glycaemic index (GI). But sourdough LAB produce organic acids that, under the heat of baking, cause interactions that reduce starch availability. The lowest-GI breads are whole-grain sourdoughs with a compact texture.

In non-scientific language, a slice of sourdough bread fills you up more than ordinary yeasted bread. This makes it more economical, especially if you bake it yourself.

So let's do it.

What's involved?

The following chapters describe how to make a sourdough starter and how to use this to make bread. There will be recipes. But it's important, from the beginning, to feel comfortable with the process. Step-by-step starter instructions are given in the next chapter. Chapter 3 describes how to use an established starter to make bread with flour, water and a little salt – nothing more.

Chapter 4 goes minimalist, with recommendations for the pared-down sourdough kitchen and the quickest slow bread imaginable: the overnight no-knead sourdough.

In Chapter 5, I answer a few frequently asked questions. Any residual worries that this whole project is going to eat up your life are dispelled in Chapter 8, which shows just how little of *your* time is actually needed, as basic schedules are given for fitting slow sourdough into hectic lives.

But for now, this is all you need:

— **Flour** (rye and/or wheat, including some wholemeal)
— **Salt**
— **Water** (tap)
— **Clean hands**
— **Scales** (digital are easiest)
— **Mixing bowl** (polypropylene, stainless steel or ceramic)
— **Bread tin or proving basket** (can be improvised)
— **Baking tray** (or baking stone)
— **Oven** (domestic, electric or gas)

Let the ferment begin.

2
Getting Started

Making sourdough bread is, normally, a three-stage process, consisting of:

— **Stage 1: Starter**
— **Stage 2: Production sourdough**
— **Stage 3: Final dough**

The starter (sometimes called 'chef', 'mother' or 'old starter') is a reservoir of useful yeasts and lactic acid bacteria that are cultured in a flour-and-water mix. Think of it as seeds waiting to be sown in the soil, i.e. in a medium where they will find the right temperature, water content and nutrients to grow. When not required to 'grow' into bread, the starter remains dormant, usually kept in the fridge.

To make bread, the starter is 'refreshed' with more than its own weight of flour and warm water. The yeasts in the starter begin to ferment, causing the dough to rise. The bacteria ferment more slowly, producing acids that flavour the dough and begin to change its structure. This is a 'production sourdough'.

After a period of several hours, a small amount of this risen production sourdough is returned to the starter pot (thus replacing what had been removed to start the process) while the rest is mixed with flour, water, salt and any other ingredients (fat, seeds, herbs, etc.) into the final dough. The whole process is described in more detail in Chapter 3. For the moment, the important points to note are:

— The starter is automatically refreshed each time you make bread
— Refreshment dilutes any accumulated acidity in the starter, so it's OK if it hasn't been used for a while
— You always keep some refreshed starter back, so the process is self-perpetuating
— Between bakes you can happily leave your starter in the fridge, undisturbed.

There are, of course, a few further details and refinements to be learned. But the basic process is really that simple.
So, let's make our starter.

> **Tip:** You can short-cut this 'make-your-own-starter' phase by getting some established starter from someone else (see Resources p. 154 for sources of dried starter and the Fungal Network of sourdough sharers). To activate a dried sourdough, dissolve it in enough warm water to make a very runny mix and then add some fresh wholemeal flour, keeping the whole thing quite sloppy. If it doesn't do much during this first refreshment, try at least one more before assuming the worst.

The key thing to remember is that you need to perform this four-day routine only *once*. Thereafter, with a viable starter up and running, you simply slot into the three-stage cycle mentioned above whenever you want to make bread.

Stage 1. Making your starter

Here are recipes for a rye starter and a wheat one.
As explained in more detail in Chapter 4, if you wish
to keep only one starter on the go I would recommend
making a rye one. Rye ferments so well and doesn't have
to be used purely for rye breads. But if wheat flour is all
that you have to hand, it will make an excellent starter too.

We'll begin with a few general principles, then the
numbers, then some hints on things to consider while
you are stirring your first mix – such as containers,
temperature, flour types, water content and so on.

Object
To give the yeasts and beneficial bacteria that occur
naturally in the flour the right conditions to ferment.

Method
Mix a small amount of flour and water in a glass jar; leave
for 24 hours, then add more flour and water and leave
for another day. Repeat on the third day and, with minor
changes, on the fourth day.

Evidence
The odd bubble may appear on the surface on day two, with
more appearing each day. Some aeration of the mixture
should be evident on the third and fourth days; this may
show as a rise in height or, if the container is transparent,
as an open honeycomb structure when the mix is viewed
side-on. It is not unusual for early evidence of bubbling to
subside, leaving a thin layer of grey liquid on the top.

Rye production sourdough

How to make a rye sourdough starter

Weigh

The quantities given in the table opposite may seem very small to start with. This is to ensure that you don't end up with so much that you throw some away. But if you want more, fine: just multiply the amounts by your chosen factor.

The grams–ounces conversion has been rounded to avoid odd numbers or fractions, so don't worry if the totals don't always add up, or the conversions are slightly different in different recipes. But, in any case, perfect accuracy isn't important here, as we are dealing with low concentrations of active ingredients.

Very helpfully, one millilitre (ml) of water weighs one gram (g) and one fluid ounce (fl oz) of water weighs one ounce (oz). It is easier to weigh small amounts of water than to measure them in a typical calibrated jug. But don't worry too much: either way will do. Bakers always adjust their water in the light of how the dough *feels*, not what the scales say.

Mix

Getting the mixture consistency right is more critical. In the case of rye flour, which is naturally sticky and highly absorbent, the starter mixture should always be sloppy, almost pourable, the texture of thin porridge. If it's too stiff, the yeast may be working, but you won't see much evidence of it.

Always mix your starter with your fingers (having washed them in clean water without too much soap or any sinister 'sanitisers'). There is good evidence that one of the key sourdough bacteria, *Lactobacillus sanfranciscensis*, isn't present in flour but gets into starters through contact with the hands of bakers.

Rye sourdough starter

Time	Ingredient	Weight	
		grams	oz
Day 1	Wholemeal rye flour	25	1
	Water (35°C/95°F)	50	2
	Total	**75**	**3**
Day 2	From previous day	75	3
	Wholemeal rye flour	25	1
	Water (35°C/95°F)	50	2
	Total	**150**	**6**
Day 3	From previous day	150	6
	Wholemeal rye flour	25	1
	Water (35°C/95°F)	50	2
	Total	**225**	**9**
Day 4	From previous day	225	9
	Wholemeal rye flour	50	2
	Water (35°C/95°F)	50	2
	Total	**325**	**13**

Starter Housekeeping

General advice on handling starters of all kinds.

Store

A glass jam or preserving jar with a screw-top lid or metal clips is suitable, but beware of a build-up of gas pressure if you fasten the lid too tightly. A good seal will help keep out unwanted moulds and contaminants. However, if no gas can escape until you open the jar, it may come out with some force. Polypropylene tubs with clip-on lids are good, especially the (relatively) tall and narrow ones, which make it easy to see how a starter is growing. Even a humble plastic bowl covered with a polythene bag will do fine.

Some space is needed for the starter to expand. Rye, once it gets going, can erupt to more than twice its starting volume. But, in general, try not to have too much air space between the top of your starter dough and the lid of the container. The oxygen in this space will help mould grow on the drying surface of the dough and on isolated smears of dough up the side walls.

Warmth

Starters need warmth to get going well. Once they are established, they can cope with all sorts of temperatures; in fact, heat is one of our key controllers. But for the first few days, like many young organisms, they do better in a warm place. We're talking 25–30°C/77–86°F, even a touch warmer for rye. This isn't always easy to achieve.

Place

In an airing cupboard (next to a hot-water tank), near a radiator or above a range cooker are all possible places. A plant propagator or heat mat can work well, especially if there's a variable heat controller (and you have a thermometer). Great results have been achieved with a hot-water bottle and a duvet.

One word of warning: never put your starter tub in full sun or directly on to a stove top, radiator or heat mat. Yeast is killed at about 60°C and you may 'cook' the bottom of your starter. Place your tub or jar on a thick cork or wooden mat and it will be fine.

But don't fret if you can't reach 25°C. Go with what you've got. Use warm (up to 35°C) water each day and keep your starter out of draughts (which cool things down greatly). The worst that can happen is that it takes a little longer for the fermentation to get going. But it will.

Flours

More or less any flour will ferment if mixed with warm water and left for a while. But starters will get going much better if the flour is all wholemeal or includes some. This is because the outer bran layers of the grain are heavily populated with yeasts and are therefore an important factor in the metabolism of lactic acid bacteria. Wholemeal rye flour (often called 'dark' rye) is teeming with yeasts and microbes. Its refined 'light' counterpart takes much longer to ferment.

Wholemeal flour is the whole wheat grain ground up with nothing removed. It is often referred to as 'wholewheat', particularly in the USA. The term 'wholegrain' is increasingly used. When applied to flour, it means the same as 'wholemeal' or 'wholewheat'. Sadly, some industrial flour sold as 'wholewheat' or 'wholemeal' is in fact reconstituted from the fractions of the wheat grain that are separated in the process of roller-milling white flour. Often, the vital wheatgerm (a source of vitamin E and other nutrients) is not put back into this not-very-wholewheat flour. Consider instead a stoneground flour, in which the germ is evenly dispersed throughout the meal.

Above all, choose organic flour. Almost all non-organic grain is sprayed with fungicides. Residues are, according to government statistics, found in a significant proportion of non-organic UK flour. Yeast is a form of fungus. Fungicides are yeast-killers.

Worse, maybe, is the widespread use of glyphosate, a weedkiller, on cereals just before harvest (to help dry out the straw). Residues of glyphosate can have harmful effects even at very low concentrations. Use organic flour to maximise the biological integrity of your starter in its most sensitive early days.

Water

Tap water is treated with chlorine, a powerful biocide, which isn't great for the bacteria that we want to nurture. There are two ways to reduce the chlorine threat: leave a jug of water standing overnight and most of the residual chlorine will evaporate; or use still spring water from a bottle. Once a starter is up and running, it will cope with water straight from the tap. Using a little spring water for the first few days will give your starter the best possible chances and won't cost much.

Wheat sourdough starter

Time	Ingredient	grams	oz
Day 1	Wholewheat (wholemeal) flour	30	1
	Water (35°C/95°F)	30	1
	Total	**60**	**2**
Day 2	From previous day	60	2
	Wholewheat (wholemeal) flour	30	1
	Water (35°C/95°F)	30	1
	Total	**120**	**4**
Day 3	From previous day	120	4
	Wholewheat (wholemeal) flour	30	1
	Water (35°C/95°F)	15	0.5
	Total	**165**	**5.5**
Day 4	From previous day	165	5.5
	White or wholewheat flour	90	3
	Water (35°C/95°F)	45	1.5
	Total	**300**	**10**

On the third and fourth days the water to flour ratio drops in order to firm the dough up a bit. It is best to keep starters very sloppy for the first few days because this is a 'mobile' environment in which biological reactions can proceed relatively quickly. It's easier to see if anything is happening if the dough is wet enough to bubble.

At the other extreme, reducing the water content of a starter to the point where it is quite dry will halt biological activity almost completely – a good tip if you want to store some starter for an extended period, perhaps to take it with you on a long journey when there will be no chance to refresh it.

Rye starters intended for regular use should always be kept pretty runny. With wheat and spelt, there is a bit more leeway. I find handling a wheat starter rather easier when it is nearer to the consistency of the dough it is going to raise, i.e. fairly firm and certainly not pourable. But there is nothing wrong with keeping a wheat starter 'liquid'.

Progress check

If you have followed the instructions above reasonably accurately, you will have a four-day-old starter which is ready to use for the first time to make bread. It will be bubbling merrily, full of life, teeming with yeasts and lactic acid bacteria, and giving off a pleasantly fruity-vinegary aroma.

Or not.

It may look a little flat, with a few surface lumps that hardly deserve the name 'bubbles'. It may have a suspicious-looking grey liquid swilling about on top. And the odour may be anything but alluring.

Beauty is in the eye of the beholder, of course, and it may take a while for the new arrival in your kitchen to grow on you (though not literally, with any luck). But one thing can be pretty safely asserted:

YOUR STARTER HASN'T DIED.

You may be wracked by guilt and feelings of failure, but steady on: such emotions are surely needed elsewhere in your life and shouldn't be frittered away on a ferment. So here's what is likely to be happening with your starter and what to do next.

Inactive starters

If we rule out the rare possibility of some fatal contamination (fungicide in the non-organic flour, or a residue of cleaning fluid on the surface of the starter bowl, for instance), the most likely reason for a starter appearing moribund is excess acidity. In other words, your starter has fermented *too* well, too quickly.

The ecology of a sourdough involves a relationship between yeasts, enzymes and bacteria that is symbiotic. They depend on each other for the provision of energy sources and 'cleansing services'. It is known, for example, that sourdough lactic acid bacteria produce not only 'bacteriocins' that knock out competing and (to humans) potentially harmful bacteria, but also anti-fungal compounds that inhibit mould growth while not unduly damaging the yeasts needed to lighten our loaves.

The relationship of the sourdough components is also dynamic. The 'wild' yeasts that inhabit our flour-water mix can tolerate the acid environment that is gradually created by the bacteria, but only up to a point. When the dough gets too fruity, the yeasts slow down and eventually stop working.

If, for whatever reason, the acids produced by the bacteria build up in the dough quickly, the yeasts will be unable to produce enough carbon dioxide gas to make much impression. It will appear as though the dough is neither bubbling nor rising. And yeast *reproduction* will be slowed or inhibited, too.

Fortunately, all that is required to revive yeast activity is to dilute the acidity of the dough. This is where the process of refreshment is so crucial. It's no good 'feeding' a dormant and over-acid starter with small amounts of flour and water. This won't be enough to correct the acidity that is the main yeast inhibitor. What is needed is a thorough refreshment with a small amount of starter and a much larger amount of fresh flour and water. This refreshment does three things:

1. It automatically dilutes the acidity of the starter and creates a neutral environment in which yeasts can work again
2. It adds, in the fresh flour component, many new yeasts and bacteria that swell the population of active agents in the sourdough
3. It provides new sources of energy for the growing population of yeasts and bacteria

Refreshing a sluggish starter

We'll use the rye starter as an example because the 'bulking up', and hence the dilution of excess acidity, is dramatic. But the same general principle holds true for a wheat sourdough (see next chapter).

Intermediate refreshment (rye starter)

Ingredients	Weight	
	grams	oz
Rye starter (old)	30	1
Wholemeal (dark) rye flour	90	3
Water (35°C/95°F)	180	6
Total	**300**	**10**

Method

Stir up the old starter to disperse any liquid on the surface.

Put half the water in a clean bowl and add 30g (1oz) of the starter. Stir to dissolve this then add all the flour. Work the mix with your fingers until any lumps have disappeared. Then add the remainder of the water, and mix until completely incorporated.

Cover with a lid or poly bag and leave in a warm place, out of draughts, for 12 to 24 hours.

If all goes to plan, the refreshed starter will show obvious signs of life. After several hours, it should be frothing on the surface (signs of the yeast fermentation) and it may well double in volume or more. By the end of the period (16 hours is a typical cycle in bakeries, but it's not critical), any eruption will probably have fallen back and the bubbles on the surface of the dough will be smaller and fewer in number.

What should it smell like? 'Pleasantly fruity and slightly acidic with hints of beer and vinegar' might be the verdict of a seasoned sourdougher. But if you're new to the process, don't be put off by what may be an unfamiliar odour. Give it the benefit of the doubt, log it in your mental aroma database for future reference and allow the proof of the pudding to be in the eating. There is more advice on dealing with reluctant starters in the troubleshooting section in Chapter 5.

If you have followed the instructions above more or less to the letter, you will now have 300 grams of refreshed starter, plus 295 grams of your original starter. The numbers may be a little lower than this because water evaporates and dough gets stuck to hands and bowls and is variously depleted. But the sourdough is certainly accumulating.

Keep your old and refreshed starters separate for the moment. Use the latter to make bread with as soon as you have time, remembering that this is still a *starter*, some of which will need to be refreshed again to make a proper production sourdough.

If you make the basic rye bread described in Chapter 8, you will use only 50 grams of your refreshed starter for this purpose. At that point you will be left with over 500 grams of residual starter – from the four-day build-up phase plus the intermediate refreshment.

Mix the two together and leave this composite starter in the fridge until you next want to make bread. No 'feeds'. No fuss. It will get more and more acidic, which is just what's needed to keep it stable and mould-free for as long as you want. Just one thing: *label your starter pot clearly*. Curious, tidy-minded, fastidious, well-meaning, but ultimately unenlightened family members and friends have been known to throw out anonymous fridge residents that appear to have 'gone off'.

Spare starter

Such risks aside, there's never any reason to chuck out accumulations of 'old' but serviceable sourdough. Apart from using some to initiate your next production sourdough, here are two positive ways to deal with any spare.

1. Pass it on. Give a little starter to someone and they can make sourdough too.

2. Use it as a natural bread 'improver'. A small amount (up to 10 per cent of total dough weight) of old starter will improve almost any bread, especially 'straight' yeasted doughs that don't involve any sponge, sourdough or long fermentation. Just mix the old starter in with all the other ingredients and enjoy the improvement to dough structure, flavour and keeping quality that comes from its rich store of organic acids.

Summary

Establishing a vigorous, well-flavoured and reliable starter is the vital first stage in making successful sourdough bread. As we've seen, it is a fairly simple process and success is likely if you understand the basic underlying biological reactions and don't confuse yourself (or your starter) with unnecessary interventions.

Good. You've nurtured a starter into a state of readiness. Time for bread.

Sourdough ciabatta

3
**Your First
Sourdough
Bread**

With a viable starter ready, Stage 1 of the sourdough bread process is complete. To turn this starter into bread, we must refresh it to increase its size and trigger a renewed fermentation which lasts several hours. Most of this mixture or 'production sourdough' is then used to make bread, with a little being kept back as the starter for the next batch of bread.

The diagram opposite shows the three stages of sourdough bread making.

Preparation

Before starting the refreshment process, it pays to work out rough timings. Sourdough takes time to do, but not too much of *your* time, unless you've rushed ahead without planning. Detailed timetables are described in Chapter 8. For now, it's enough to note that, for our first wheat bread, fermenting the production sourdough will take at least four hours and the final rise will take up to five hours.

The 3 stages of sourdough bread making

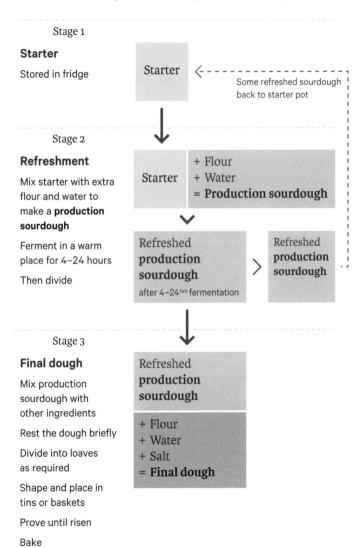

Stage 1

Starter

Stored in fridge

Starter

Some refreshed sourdough
back to starter pot

Stage 2

Refreshment

Mix starter with extra
flour and water to
make a **production
sourdough**

Ferment in a warm
place for 4–24 hours

Then divide

Starter + Flour
+ Water
= **Production sourdough**

Refreshed **production sourdough** after 4–24 hrs fermentation

Refreshed **production sourdough**

Stage 3

Final dough

Mix production
sourdough with
other ingredients

Rest the dough briefly

Divide into loaves
as required

Shape and place in
tins or baskets

Prove until risen

Bake

Refreshed **production sourdough**

+ Flour
+ Water
+ Salt
= **Final dough**

Equipment needed

This is what you'll need. As you can see, a bit of improvisation is fine if you don't have everything to hand.

Sourdough starter

Mixing bowl – 4-litre (4 US quarts) capacity, stainless steel, polypropylene, ceramic or wood

Baking tin(s) or
Proving basket(s) – to support the dough while it is rising; can be any of the following:
— Wicker basket lined with (usually sewn-in) linen – the classic French *banneton* (or *paneton* for the purists)
— Bent cane basket (called *brotform* in German – see photo)
— Compressed wood-pulp basket, with smooth, ridged or patterned interior
— Any old basket (loaf-shaped is good) lined with a cloth, preferably of an open weave like linen or hemp and fairly thick

Baking tray (if baking a free-standing loaf) lined with non-stick baking parchment or silicone mat *or*

Baking stone – pre-heat in an electric or gas domestic oven for that 'brick-oven-bottom' effect

Large, strong poly bag to cover the rising dough.
Can be washed and re-used many times. (Cling-film, or cling-wrap, is best avoided. It is single-use and therefore wasteful, and it often 'clings' to dough just when you'd rather it didn't.)

Dough scraper

Flour, preferably organic and stoneground

Sea salt

Simple sourdough wheat bread

Makes one large or two small loaves

Refresh the starter

This is the moment when your starter comes to life again. It may have been used quite recently, or it may have been sitting in the fridge for a while. Either way, this refreshment will achieve two main things:

1. It will show how much life there is in your starter
2. It will produce sufficient vigorously fermenting dough to act as the 'raising agent' in your final dough

Stage 2. Production sourdough

Ingredients	Weight	
	grams	oz
Wheat starter	150	5
Wholemeal/wholewheat flour	100	3.5
White/light bread flour	100	3.5
Water (35°C/95°F)	120	4
Total	**470**	**16**

Note

The flour for the production sourdough doesn't necessarily have to be particularly 'strong', i.e. high in gluten proteins. As long as it is above 10% protein and includes some 'brown' flour containing the active wheatgerm and bran, it will do the job well.

Wheat production sourdough

Method

1. If there is any liquid on the surface of your starter, give it a quick stir. Then take 150g (5oz) and break it up with 120g (4oz) of warm water. The starter will be cold from the fridge, so this water needs to be around the 35–40°C mark (it's worth using a thermometer). If it's much less than that, and if the flour is quite cool too, the production sourdough will take longer than normal to ferment. (On the other hand, as we will see later, deliberately using cool water is a way of extending the fermentation period of the production sourdough so that it's ready to take to the next stage at a time to suit your schedule.)

2. Add the flour and mix until the dough comes together. Then tip it out onto the table and give it a very brief knead – about 30 seconds – just to get rid of any lumps.

3. Cover the bowl with a polythene bag and leave it in a warm place, out of draughts (see p. 26 for suggestions), for 4 hours. This is a rough guide to how long a production sourdough takes to develop. Signs of healthy life are:

   — The dough should rise as the yeasts begin to work, at least doubling in volume.
   — If you're using a transparent bowl, hold it at eye level and the aeration will be visible as the dough takes on a honeycomb structure.

Not sure?

Until you've done it a few times, judging the 'ripeness' of a production sourdough can cause anxiety, so let's quickly think things through.

Fermentation is very dependent on temperature. A difference of 5°C can halve or double the time taken by a given cycle of fermentation (i.e. for your dough to rise). So, if it hasn't more or less doubled in size in four hours, the dough may simply be a bit cold. You can move it to a warmer place (if you have one), but it's just as easy to leave it where it is for a bit longer. In a cool kitchen with a young starter, it's quite possible for a production sourdough to take seven or eight hours to 'come up'.

The good news is – it's not critical.

Provided there are some signs of yeast activity and the dough has swelled a bit, you are on the right track. If leaving the production sourdough a little longer is going to mess up other plans, it's fine to press on to make the final dough. The worst that can happen is that the yeast population is a bit sparse, in which case the final rise ('proof') may take more time.

The most useful piece of advice to sourdough bakers is probably 'be patient'. We're working with natural micro-organisms at relatively low concentrations and they cannot be rushed. However, the great advantage of this slow tempo is that it gives us bigger windows to perform key actions.

Can it go the other way, with the production sourdough fermenting *too much*? Yes, but this is only likely to happen in very warm conditions and when making larger amounts of dough (because big doughs generate heat faster than they can lose it). An over-ripe production sourdough will have clearly risen in its bowl and then collapsed and may smell distinctly vinegary. Over-fermented production sourdough contains higher than usual levels of acids (lactic, acetic, butyric, ferulic, etc.) which, apart from playing an important role in flavour and nutrition, may break down the dough's gluten structure a bit too quickly for comfort. The chemistry is subtle, but to a baker an over-fermented sourdough means a ragged and hard-to-handle final dough.

Be that as it may, *slow* sourdough is a more typical 'problem'. There are more remedial suggestions in Chapter 5, but let's assume that a combination of time and patience has done the trick: the production sourdough is ready for Stage 3 of the process, making the final dough.

Stage 3. Final dough

Ingredients	Weight	
	grams	oz
Production sourdough (from above)*	300	10
Wholemeal/wholewheat flour	100	3.5
White/light bread flour	300	10
Water, lukewarm (30°C/86°F)	300	10
Sea salt	8	0.3
Total	**1008**	**34**

* If you followed the Stage 2 recipe, you'll have made 470g of production sourdough. Using 300g to make bread now will leave you with about 150g (because of residues on tubs and hands etc.) which you should put back into your starter (Stage 1) pot in the fridge.

Method

1. Make a *soaker*. This is a way of developing the gluten in the dough without kneading. Simply mix the flour, salt and water together in a bowl – do not include your production sourdough at this stage. Do this with one hand, until all the flour is wet and there are no very big lumps. It should take no more than a minute. Cover the bowl with a big polythene bag or similar. Leave for half an hour or so.

2. Turn the dough onto a worktop, using a little water (*not* flour) to 'lubricate' the surface and stop the dough sticking. As you begin to work the dough, you will notice the soaker effect: the stretchy gluten network has formed all by itself. Using both hands, fold it over, stretch it out, turn it through 90 degrees, and so on. Moisten your hands and the worktop every now and then. If any dough has stuck, scrape it off, wet the surface and carry on. The dough will get smoother and stretchier. Five minutes is all it takes.

3. Now add the production sourdough by working it into the fresh dough until it is thoroughly mixed. This may be sticky work. Scrape the dough from your fingers and, if it helps, use a little water to clean your hands, but put all the bits back in your dough, never down the sink.

4. This is the moment to adjust the water content of the dough. This recipe has a nominal 'hydration rate' (baker speak for the ratio of water to flour) of 75 per cent (300g of water to 400g of flour). That is a lot of water. Conventional yeasted doughs often have

little more than 60 per cent water to flour. But it's important: not only can the sourdough yeasts inflate a soft dough more easily than a tight one, but a wetter dough makes for a chewy, open-textured crumb. The bread will keep a bit longer, too.

5. The only downside with wet dough is its natural tendency to sag outwards on the baking tray when formed into free-standing loaves. A bit of experimentation will help you arrive at your own balance of good shape and eating quality. But it's worth remembering this: the surest way to get a 'brick' or a 'doorstep' is to make your dough too dry by adding extra flour. I say: the wetter, the better.

6. After adding the production sourdough, no more than five minutes' kneading is required. Check the dough by cutting off a piece the size of a small apple and stretching it gently between moistened fingers to see how thin it will go as you work it in all directions. This is the 'window pane' test. You are looking for a thin but unbroken layer of a cloudy, latex-like membrane of gluten. It won't be perfect and the more wholemeal in your choice of flour, the more bran and wheatgerm particles there will be to obscure the gluten. But if you make a habit of doing this test with every dough you make, you will have a scale of stretchiness and resilience on which to judge the quality of each batch.

7. Rest the dough for a few minutes (loosely covered with a poly bag) while you get a baking tin or proving basket ready. The gluten will relax and shaping the dough will be easier.

Sourdough wheat bread (before shaping)

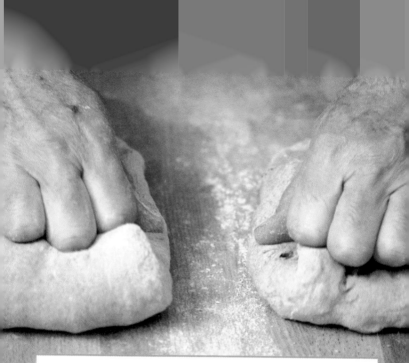

Kneading

There is no right or wrong way of kneading. Anything goes, from gentle folding and stretching to a rapid two-handed scrabbling. The purpose of kneading is to help the gluten structure to form. When energy is applied to the dough, the chains of protein molecules that make up what we call 'gluten' grow longer and stronger. The result is stretchier and smoother dough.

Here's one suggestion. Moisten your hands and the table top with a film of water to stop the dough sticking. Pull the far edge of the dough lump over towards you and then push and stretch the dough away from you with either your thumbs or the heel of your hand. Turn the dough piece through 90 degrees and repeat.

Evolving a rhythm makes the job more satisfying. If it really hurts, ease off or try a different method. Be patient – the dough will come together eventually.

Dividing, shaping, final rise

If you are making more than one loaf, divide the dough into pieces. Sourdough bread is usually proved (i.e. given its final rise) in cloth-lined baskets and baked on the oven bottom (or a stone or baking tray), but there is no reason why it shouldn't be baked in a tin. Shaping (what bakers call *moulding*) will vary according to this choice.

Tin bread is normally sliced for sandwiches or toast, so convention dictates that it should be even-textured. This means rolling the dough up quite tightly so that there are no gaps or holes. Place it carefully in the tin with any 'seam' facing downwards. The dough should come just over halfway up the sides. Don't fiddle with it once it's in the tin, however lopsided it looks. Dough naturally takes the shape of the tin and always looks better if it hasn't been primped or petted.

Proving baskets need to be dusted with flour before use – not a thick layer, but enough for some to lodge in the weave of the cloth (or the gaps between canes). The best flour by far for this purpose is *brown rice flour*. It is slightly gritty and has a ball-bearing feel. It helps release the dough from the proving cloth or basket, not least because, being gluten-free, it doesn't start to become dough when it gets moist (as per the soaker mechanism described above). If you haven't got (and can't get hold of) any rice flour, here are some alternatives, in descending order of efficacy (in the sense of preventing dough from sticking in proving baskets) and effect on the crust:

— **Cornmeal (maize meal)** – coarse and golden yellow, so can look good on the loaf; gluten-free; not to be confused with cornflour which is highly refined and too fine for this job

for
Bread

Russian sourdough rye bread

- **Semolina** – derived from wheat and will go a bit sticky when wet, but usefully coarse

- **Wheat bran** – no gluten-forming element, so good 'release' properties; can give loaf a pronounced rough surface and rather 'worthy' crust

- **Wholemeal wheat flour** – usually coarse enough to do a reasonable job, but contains gluten so will go sticky when wet enough

- **White flour** – easy to spread and fine enough to cling to cloth and basket surfaces; will form gluten and go sticky when wet; some danger of 'caking' and a dry powdery crust if used in excess.

Put your dusting flour in a shallow bowl or in a low pile on the worktop. Gather the dough piece by gently folding it in on itself so that at least one side is smooth and free of cracks and folds. Holding the dough with one hand, roll this smooth side in the bowl or pile of flour to cover as much as possible of the surface with a thin layer.

Pick the dough piece up from the sides (i.e. don't lift it from underneath and risk folding dry flour into the interior of the loaf) and place it gently in the prepared proving basket. Check that there is no wet dough sticking to the basket and dust any moist surfaces with a quick flick of flour.

Cover the tin or basket loosely, making sure that nothing can get stuck to the dough during the final rise. Put it in a warm place out of draughts.

Under normal conditions (i.e. the kind that rarely actually prevail), this dough should be ready for the oven in four to five hours. How will you know? It will have risen noticeably, though the proverbial 'doubling in size' will be more obvious in a tin than a basket. Final confirmation comes from the fingers: press gently on the risen dough with the soft 'pad' of your middle finger and note the resilience, or lack of it, in the dough. If it feels quite firm and springs back readily, it may need a little longer.

If it feels delicate and in danger of caving in under your finger without bouncing back, it is already over-proved and should be baked as soon as possible.

Into the oven

Tin loaves can go straight into the oven, pre-heated to 230°C (see Oven Temperature Conversion Chart on p. 153), or even 240°C if your oven allows.

For any type of bread, reduce the oven temperature setting by 20–30°C (about 36–54°F) after about ten minutes' baking. If you ask your oven to carry on belting out maximum heat, the crust of the loaf will probably burn. In any kind of 'retained heat' oven, such as a wood-fired brick oven, the temperature drops gradually during baking as the available heat energy is 'consumed' by the baking process. Turning the controls down a bit after a few minutes goes some way to emulating the conditions in a brick oven.

Is it baked?

Ovens vary enormously, so treat any baking times as only a guide. The action of baking bread in a hot oven is to form a crust as soon as possible on all the exposed surfaces of the loaf. Once formed, the crust acts like a heat shield and waterproof jacket all in one. It protects the inside of the loaf from exposure to the full heat of the oven which would otherwise try to form a 'crust' out of the whole thing. It also stops some of the steam escaping from the middle of the loaf. Much of the water used in making the dough is turned to steam as the loaf warms up in the oven. Since steam cannot (at atmospheric pressure) get hotter than 100°C, it in effect *cools* the middle of the loaf (known as the 'crumb'). In fact the centre of a fully baked loaf never exceeds about 96°C even though it may be only millimetres away from an oven temperature of 220°C. This explains why crust and crumb are such different results of the same initial process.

A loaf is fully baked when all the internal crumb has been turned from soft wet dough to something firmer, in which starches have been gelatinised and water has evaporated. This may take **40 to 50 minutes** for a 1kg (2lb) loaf in a domestic oven, rather less if the loaves are smaller. Here is a checklist of questions to ask and things to look for in judging whether a loaf is baked:

— Has it been in the oven for a credible amount of time? If it's taking a lot of colour after ten minutes, it may look baked, but it very probably won't be cooked inside.
— Is it evenly coloured – top, bottom and sides?
— Are the sides (of tin loaves), near where the top crust begins, as firm as the rest of the crust? This is the last place where softness lingers. See if you can push a thumbnail through: if you can easily, the loaf needs a bit longer in the oven.
— When you press hard down on the top crust (of free-standing loaves), does the crust give at all? If it does, the loaf isn't done properly yet.
— When you tap it on the bottom, does it sound hollow? (This is a traditional, but not a very reliable, test because even a slightly under-baked loaf can sound hollow.)
— Finally (one for the techies), has the centre of the crumb reached 95°C (about 200°F) when measured with a digital probe? If it's significantly lower, best bake on for a bit longer.

Congratulations!

You've baked some real sourdough bread.

Cool it on a wire rack so that it doesn't sweat. Try to let it cool to room temperature before tasting it. That way, it's easier to cut and has more flavour. You're also less likely to wolf down quite so many slices in one sitting.

Once it's cool, keep it in a polythene bag. This will conserve moisture, which begins to migrate from crumb to crust (thereby softening it) as soon as the loaf is out of the oven. To re-crisp a flabby crust, put the loaf in a moderate oven for five minutes.

If your free-standing loaf 'pancaked' a bit as it baked, don't despair. Judge it on its inner qualities, not just on the shape of its curves. If someone complains about long shallow chunks not making very good sandwiches, hold the loaf at a 45-degree angle and watch beautiful oval slices fall from your knife.

All bread freezes well and it's a good plan to slice the loaf beforehand. It makes defrosting quicker and, by taking a few slices at a time, you can enjoy almost-fresh bread (without the industrial enzymes and preservatives, of course) whenever you wish, with no waste.

If you allow your bread to age naturally, it can be enjoyed in so many ways – seven, at least, as suggested on pp. 132–5. You may notice, as the days pass, a little-known facet of sourdough bread: its flavour improves each day. Not so surprising, since we all appreciate the way other fermented foods and drinks mature. Roll on the day when bakers charge more for well-aged sourdough bread!

Time management

The recipe and instructions in this chapter are for a straightforward sourdough loaf, in which the fermentation has taken place at room temperature, more or less. Made this way, the whole process takes 10 to 12 hours from start to finish, or a little more if your starter is young and your kitchen cool.

That, of course, is the total elapsed time. Your involvement, the amount of time when you are actually making the bread to the exclusion of everything else except listening to the radio, is much less. The table opposite gives a rough idea. Obviously, some people work faster than others. But it's reassuring to know that making this slow, fascinating, delicious and digestible food doesn't take all day. Well, it does ... but you know what I mean.

The whole process takes about 11 hours from start to finish. Your actual involvement is about an hour.

Mention has already been made of how temperature affects the speed of fermentation. Though often seen as a negative ('my dough won't rise', 'I have nowhere as warm as that in my flat', etc.), temperature can be made to work for us. By cooling doughs down deliberately, we can schedule those baking stages that need our involvement for times in our busy days when we can fit them in most easily.

For instance, instead of planning a four-hour slot for our Stage 2 production sourdough, it might be neater to cool it down and let it take eight or twelve hours. A sourdough refreshed in the morning before work could easily be ready to make into dough in the evening after work in Chapter 8, but for now, let's put these baking skills to good use and try out a variety of breads to suit all palates.

Bread time check

Action	Duration	Your time
	hh:mm	mins
Make production sourdough	0:10	10
Ferment production sourdough	4:00	
Weigh dough ingredients	0:05	5
Mix soaker	0:05	5
Soaker time	0:30	
Knead dough (1)	0:05	5
Add sourdough, knead dough (2)	0:10	10
Rest dough, prepare tins/baskets	0:05	5
Shape dough, put in tins/baskets	0:05	5
Final proof	5:00	
Slash, put in oven	0:05	5
Bake	0:40	
Remove from oven; tidy up	0:10	10
Total elapsed time/active time	**11:10**	**60**

Simple sourdough wheat bread

(Top to bottom)
Pumpkin and linseed sourdough bread
Sourdough pizza
Black pepper crispbread

4
One Starter,
Many Loaves

Wheat, rye, wet, dry, cool, warm, evening, dawn – the adaptability of sourdough baking is impressive. One way of reducing the many variables is to stick with just one starter. Less fridge space will be used, of course, and familiarity will soon breed contentment, as you get comfortable with the controls.

The rye starter is the clear favourite here, the one that you'd take to your desert island. It takes up less space (because the refreshment stage turns a small amount of starter into ten times as much production sourdough), it is generally more vigorous and its naturally occurring yeasts and bacteria adapt quickly to mixing with other flours.

In this chapter, we'll use our basic rye starter from Chapter 2 to make wheat and spelt breads, with various additions. Then we will reduce the process of sourdough bread-making to a sublime simplicity with a recipe that produces a loaf with a few grams of starter, a single mix and a total of about five minutes of active work. All those who have ever thought that they don't have time to make bread, let alone sourdough bread, are in for a treat.

———

Rye-wheat bread

This recipe refreshes a rye starter with wheat flour and uses the resulting production sourdough to make a basic bread. This can be baked 'as is', and is also a good 'base' for multigrain or seeded variations, two of which are described.

Note that the refreshment stage generates just enough production sourdough to make the final dough, with no extra to put back in the starter pot. This is deliberate: the production sourdough is a hybrid of wheat and rye and would 'contaminate' a pot of pure rye starter. This may not matter to you at all. But there are sound reasons for keeping starters 'pure', even if they are going to be used to make doughs with other flours. Firstly, known starters are more predictable. If you add, let's say, wheat (or other) flour to a rye starter, the 'ecology' of the system will change – not much, perhaps, but enough, in time, to affect the speed and vigour of the fermentation process, not to mention the flavour of the eventual bread. Put simply, you may lose a bit of control, especially if the starter is playing host to a constantly changing assortment of flours. Secondly, a significant number of people want to avoid wheat protein in their diet and may be particularly appreciative of your rye bread if it is just that, without any 'cross-contamination'.

If you follow this principle and make only enough production sourdough for the batch of bread that you are making now with no extra, don't let your rye starter run out. When levels in the pot in the fridge get low, simply do a small refreshment (as described in Chapter 2, p. 32) and put the whole lot back in the pot. Alternatively, when making an all-rye bread, make a bit too much production sourdough so that you have some extra to boost your stock in the fridge.

Sourdough refreshment to make a rye-wheat production sourdough

Ingredients	Weight	
	grams	oz
Rye starter (from the fridge)	75	2.5
Wholemeal wheat flour	85	3
White or light brown flour	55	2
Water (35°C/95°F)	85	3
Total	**300**	**11**

Note: 1 millilitre of water weighs 1 gram

Method

Mix everything together until reasonably smooth (about two minutes with one hand in the bowl), cover and ferment for 4 to 8 hours (longer with cooler water). The dough should rise appreciably in the bowl during this time. Ideally, take it to the next stage (i.e. make it into the final dough) when it is at its peak or shortly after. A production sourdough that has risen and collapsed several hours before you use it may be sourer than you want and may start weakening the gluten in the final dough more quickly than desirable.

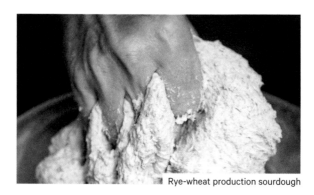

Rye-wheat production sourdough

Basic rye-wheat dough (final dough)

Makes one 1kg or two 500g plain loaves

Ingredients	Weight	
	grams	oz
Rye-wheat production sourdough	300	10
Wholemeal wheat flour	200	7
White or light brown flour	200	7
Sea salt	8	0.25
Water (30°C/80°F)	300	10
Total	**1008**	**34**

Note: 1 millilitre of water weighs 1 gram

Method

Mix the flours, salt and water together, cover and soak for half an hour. If you want to extend the final proof, make the water cooler (20°C/68°F).

Turn the 'soaker' out onto a worktop (see photo overleaf) and knead it briefly using wet hands. Add the sourdough and work it into the dough until it is completely dispersed. Knead for a few more minutes. Once the water has had a chance to be absorbed fully by the flour, check the dough consistency and add flour or water as necessary. This should be a fairly soft dough. It is mostly wheat by now and should develop into a fairly stretchy dough. Don't expect miracles of lightness, however: it is over 50 per cent wholemeal flour, so it will have a coarser feel than a purely white dough.

This dough can be baked either in a tin or on a baking tray or stone. Choose your method, divide the dough into pieces as required and shape as described in Chapter 3, p. 51.

The final rise or 'proof' will take 3 to 5 hours at normal temperatures and can be extended by making the dough cooler and proving in an unheated room.

Bake at the usual sort of temperature for a plain unsweetened bread, i.e. starting at 230°C and dropping to 210°C after 10 minutes or so. Bake time depends on the oven, but is likely to be around 35 to 40 minutes for a large loaf, 25 to 30 minutes for a half-sized one.

Pumpkin and linseed sourdough

Multigrain bread

Makes two 750g (26oz) loaves

Prepare the following 'soaker' a day in advance.

Multigrain soaker

Ingredients	Weight	
	grams	oz
Chopped ('kibbled') rye grain	125	4
Pot barley grain, kibbled wheat, pinhead oatmeal, or other whole grain	125	4
Hot water (recently boiled)	250	8
Total	**500**	**16**

Note: 1 millilitre of water weighs 1 gram

Method

Pour the hot water onto the grains, stir up into a mash, cover and leave for 24 hours.

Add the grain mash to the plain rye-wheat dough (recipe p. 65) in the ratio 500g (16oz) dough to 250g (8oz) soaker. You can, of course, use less or more soaker if you wish to vary the 'heartiness' of the bread.

Knead the dough as described on p. 65. Any operation that involves folding and stretching a dough with a significant wheat gluten element is made easier by waiting a short time. So leave it, loosely covered, for a few minutes to allow the gluten to relax. Pull the dough gently out into a flat pillow and spread the grain mash over the top. Fold one end over and roll the whole thing up into a Swiss roll. Turn it through 90 degrees, flatten it with your hand and roll it up again. Two or three more turns should see the grains well dispersed throughout the dough. Use a little water on the table and your hands to prevent the dough sticking, and be gentle: if you push too hard, you will end up with a dog's dinner, with grains flying everywhere.

Divide the dough into two equal pieces. Leave them for a minute or two (to allow the gluten to relax again) and then shape them as required. For tin loaves, roll the dough up fairly firmly, using a flick of flour on the table if necessary. For basket-proved loaves, the final shaping doesn't have to be as tight, but make sure that you present a reasonably smooth surface to the rice flour (or similar) in which you dip the dough piece before placing it gently in the proving basket. It doesn't matter what the top surface looks like at this stage because it will become the bottom of the baked loaf, but try to avoid folding dry flour into the dough as this can result in pasty streaks disfiguring the baked crumb.

Cover the loaves loosely with poly bags and prove in a place away from draughts. At room temperature this will take between 4 and 8 hours, depending on the combination of factors discussed above – temperature, wetness of dough and the vitality of the sourdough. You may notice that loaves such as these with a high proportion of 'bits' (in this case the grains) in them take longer to prove than their plain counterparts. Two factors may be at work here. First, the grains themselves do not become aerated and expand like the dough, so they act as a 'dead weight' that the rest of the dough has to carry. Second, even though the grain mash may feel soft and moist, it has a firming effect on the dough structure, making it hold together better and therefore expand more reluctantly. As the old expression goes, 'You can't make bricks without straw' – when bricks were made of mud, straw was necessary to stiffen the mix. In baking terms, this helps to explain why breads composed almost entirely of larger pieces of grain – pumpernickel, for instance – are usually much less crumbly than plain loaves.

Bake as for any unsweetened bread, starting fairly hot and turning the heat down by 20°C (see Conversion Chart on p. 153) after 10 minutes or so. About 35 to 40 minutes should do it, depending on oven conditions.

Multigrain sourdough bread

Pumpkin and linseed bread

This is the same idea as the multigrain bread, only with seeds. Linseeds (flax seeds) have a notable 'binding' quality in addition to their important nutritional properties (fibre and a good source of essential fatty acids such as omega-3). When soaked in water they look rather like frog-spawn, but when baked they impart a delicious nutty, slightly oily quality to the bread.

Seed soaker

Ingredients	Weight	
	grams	oz
Linseeds (golden or brown)	125	4
Pumpkin seeds	125	4
Hot water (recently boiled)	250	8
Total	**500**	**16**

Note: 1 millilitre of water weighs 1 gram

Method

Pour hot water onto the seeds, stir up into a mash, cover and leave for 24 hours.

Add 250g (8oz) of the seed soaker to 500g (16oz) of the plain rye-wheat dough, following the instructions for the multigrain bread (p. 67) all the way through.

Assembling the pumpkin and linseed sourdough bread

Spelt sourdough

Spelt is a baking phenomenon. Almost the same (according to the scientists) as its modern counterpart wheat, it is being chosen by more and more people, despite its much higher cost, because it is easier to digest. The rise of spelt is a triumph of what might be called citizen science. Instead of waiting for the placebo-controlled, randomised trials without which, we are told, no valid conclusions can be drawn about what food does to us, people have conducted their own 'feeding trials'. Treating this ancient grain as a culinary opportunity, they have found it to be more digestible than ordinary wheat and the word has spread. Most artisan and micro-bakers include spelt loaves in their assortment. It goes down well – in every sense.

What has this got to do with sourdough? The answer is in the way spelt ferments. We must set aside as unproven one explanation for spelt's evident digestibility – the fact that it is never used to make industrial loaves, the theory being that any difference between wheat and spelt may simply be down to the additives, declared or hidden, that are integral to high-speed processing. Almost all spelt bread is indeed made by small bakeries who take longer over their dough and often use sourdough methods. And, as any baker will tell you, spelt flour ferments well. There isn't space here to go into the reasons, but spelt seems to be a powerhouse of both micro-nutrients and micro-organisms. The latter, the natural yeasts and bacteria present on the grain and therefore in the flour, ferment vigorously and, in doing so, help create the conditions for our digestive systems to absorb useful amounts of nutrients. This process requires sourdough in order to give of its best.

From the baker's point of view, spelt can be a little tricky to control. In any given recipe, expect it to ferment in between half and three-quarters of the time taken by a wheat-flour dough. Watch out, too, for how the spelt gluten structure softens and begins to break down more quickly than wheat. In practice, this boils down to some simple guidelines for spelt sourdough breads:

— Shorten the fermentation period of the production sourdough or use cooler water, or both.
— Make the final spelt dough cooler than usual unless a quick proof is what you want.
— Err on the side of under-proof, because the dough can collapse if left too long.

The recipe that follows involves a short-cut. Instead of starting a spelt sourdough from scratch (which can be done by substituting spelt flour for wheat in the recipe in Chapter 2), we use the ever-reliable rye starter.

This recipe will make one large or two small loaves.

Spelt sourdough with walnuts

Rye-spelt production sourdough

Ingredients	Weight	
	grams	oz
Rye sourdough starter	50	2
Spelt flour (wholemeal)	150	6
Water (22–25°C/72–77°F)	100	4
Total	**300**	**12**

Note: 1 millilitre of water weighs 1 gram

Method

The rye starter can come straight from the fridge and does not have to have been refreshed recently. Disperse it in the lukewarm water, add the spelt flour and mix to a soft dough. Cover and leave for 3 to 4 hours, during which time the dough should rise noticeably.

Spelt sourdough bread

Ingredients	Weight	
	grams	oz
Rye-spelt production sourdough (from above)	275	9.5
Spelt flour (wholemeal)	450	16
Sea salt	8	0.25
Water (22–25°C/72–77°F)	275	9.5
Total	**1008**	**35**

Note: 1 millilitre of water weighs 1 gram

Method

Make a soaker on the fly by mixing the spelt flour, water and salt together and leaving covered for half an hour. Turn out onto a table top and knead briefly.

Add the production sourdough. Knead the complete dough briefly as the acids from the production sourdough begin to work on the gluten. Don't go on too long, as this dough can begin to break down quite rapidly. If you get the feeling that the dough is beginning to tear even without undue kneading pressure, stop immediately. As with any dough, adjust the water or flour content to achieve the desired dough consistency – in this case a fairly soft one.

Handling doughs that are very tacky on the surface can be difficult. If you are going to bake the loaf in a tin, I would recommend handling it with wet hands and on a wet table before putting it in the tin. If you are proving in a basket, you'll need to pick the dough piece up in a lump and gently dip it in a bowl of flour to coat the surface of the dough that is going to come into contact with the basket (which you will have pre-floured too). If you cannot pick up the dough piece at all, it is too soft and you should add just enough flour to make it possible to handle as one lump. But, having said that, the softer the dough, the better the eating and keeping quality will be.

Rest for five minutes or so (the dough, that is). Divide if necessary, then shape and place into a tin or proving basket. Proof will usually take a little less time than for a wheat dough, say 3 to 4 hours at room temperature. Judge when it is ready for the oven not by what the clock says but by the state of the dough, which should have roughly doubled in volume and, when pressed gently with your middle finger, should feel puffy and still slightly springy.

Bake for around 40 minutes, starting at 230°C and dropping to 210°C after 10 minutes or so.

Spelt sourdough with walnuts

This is a simple variation of the basic spelt bread. Walnuts go well with sourdough bread and the combination appears in the French repertoire as the much-loved *pain aux noix*. There are a couple of points to note:

— Soaking walnuts overnight softens their often dry skins and restores to the flesh that wonderful buttery texture of freshly harvested nuts.
— Walnuts bleed a purple-tinted dye, especially in an acid sourdough, so don't work the dough longer than the minimum after adding the nuts, otherwise a pleasant streaky effect will give way to a rather dull dark coloration of the dough.

Walnut soaker

Ingredients	Weight	
	grams	oz
Walnuts (pieces)	150	5
Hot water (recently boiled)	75	2.5
Total	**225**	**8**

Note: 1 millilitre of water weighs 1 gram

Method

Pour the hot water onto the nuts, swirl around, cover and leave for 24 hours.

To every 400g (14oz) of spelt sourdough bread dough, add 100g (3.5oz) of soaked nuts. Some of the water evaporates overnight, so the above quantities should yield enough for one large loaf or two small ones.

Fold the nuts carefully into a slightly relaxed final dough. Don't worry too much about evenness of distribution. Shape and place in a suitable tin (or basket). Prove and bake as for the plain version, except that any dough with nuts is more prone to taking too much colour (in other words, burning), so drop the oven temperature by 10–15°C all round.

The breads just described show how a plain rye starter can be used to make a variety of breads with other flours without any complicated 'feeding' or 'building' protocols. For sheer simplicity, however, the next bread cannot be outdone.

So let's throw away the rule book and harness the extraordinary power of time and sourdough to make the ultimate slow bread for busy people.

Overnight no-knead sourdough bread

Overnight No-knead Sourdough

Ingredients	Weight	
	grams	oz
Rye starter (old)	5	0.2
Wholemeal wheat flour	150	5
White wheat flour	450	16
Sea salt	8	0.25
Water (22–25°C/72–77°F)	400	14
Total	**1013**	**35**

Note: 1 millilitre of water weighs 1 gram

That's not a misprint: only 5 grams (about a level teaspoon or a pea-sized piece) of sourdough starter is needed. It doesn't have to be fresh, but it is best from a source that has already proved itself in action, as it were. If you are using a relatively young starter, increase the amount to 10 grams.

Method
Mix the starter (straight from the fridge is fine) with the warm water and add the flour and salt. Mix in a bowl until all the flour is wet, turn the dough out onto the table and work it for a minute until any lumps have gone. This is not really kneading, just a thorough mixing, and it should take no longer than a minute, or two at the most. Note that this is a pretty wet dough (75 per cent hydration). It needs to be, to allow the very small initial number of yeast cells to multiply and 'pump' enough carbon dioxide gas to raise the dough without too much resistance from a tight gluten structure.

Gather the dough into as smooth a lump as you can and either place it in a prepared tin or dunk it in brown rice flour and put it in a proving basket.

Place the tin or basket in a large polythene bag which can be slightly inflated (like blowing up a balloon) in order to prevent contact with the dough. Leave it at room temperature for a couple of hours if possible and then transfer to a cooler place (10–12°C/50–54°F) for 16 hours or so. Unless the loaf has risen fully by this time, bring it back into a warm place to finish proving. Timing will depend, as usual, on the vigour of the starter and the actual temperature prevailing. It may take longer than 20 hours in total. In fact, it can be rather convenient if it takes about 24 hours to rise fully. That way, you could make it mid-evening one day and bake it mid-evening the next.

The fully proved dough will be pretty fragile, so take care when turning it out of a proving basket, or be careful not to knock the tin on the way to the oven.

Baking temperature and time is much the same as for any plain loaf such as the basic wheat sourdough bread in Chapter 3, so 40 to 50 minutes for a 1kg loaf and a bit less for half-size ones. Start at 230°C (or as high as your oven will go) and turn the heat down by 20°C after 10 minutes' baking.

What, no production sourdough?

As you will have spotted, this is an all-in-one process. It goes straight from Stage 1, the starter, to Stage 3, the final dough. Apart from saving time and complication, this has some implications that are worth noting:

— We are, in effect, making a slow production sourdough with a bit of salt in it and then baking it. The proportion of starter is tiny (less than 0.5 per cent) compared to 10 per cent for a normal rye production sourdough and 30 per cent for a wheat one. Apart from anything else, this shows the remarkable ability of a small amount of starter to 'inoculate' a much bigger mass of flour and water. It gives a feeling of 'almost anything is possible' and is worth remembering if, for instance, you find yourself short of starter any time.

— It takes a long time for the yeast cells to multiply to the point where there are enough of them to make their presence felt in raising the dough. This gives the naturally slower lactic acid bacteria sufficient time to do their thing, which is to produce (mainly) lactic and acetic acids. These give this long-process bread a very distinct tangy flavour and (though it may scarcely be relevant) excellent keeping qualities: its crumb remains quite supple and it will stay mould-free for much longer than a normal loaf.

So that's it. A sourdough loaf that takes a day to develop but only a few minutes of your time to make. Sorted, as they say.

Or are we?

Success with sourdough has a lot to do with knowing what you are looking for – and at. One person's terminally inactive gloop is another person's reliable starter. The difference between failure and success, despair and hope, need be no more than a little patient observation and informed analysis – with maybe a nod to the underlying science. All of which is provided in the Frequently Asked Questions about sourdough in Chapter 5, which are a prelude to more simple and delicious recipes in Chapter 6.

5

‘Have I Killed
My Starter?’ …
and other FAQ

Let's admit it, sourdough has a bit of an image problem. The name doesn't help, for a start. The French *levain* is all upbeat and positive, but our sourdough sounds a bit 'off' and unappetising. And, although sourdough obviously comes to life from time to time, it soon reverts, like an ageing pet, to a state of slightly whiffy inactivity.

But, of course, sourdough shouldn't be judged by external appearances at all. It's what's going on *inside* that matters. And that's the problem. What *is* going on? Is *anything* going on?

This chapter is for anyone who has ever asked such questions and not found an answer. Sourdough bread-making is, I insist, essentially very simple, but there are plenty of things that can go wrong (or look as though they are going wrong). The good news is that most can be fixed easily if you know what to look for.

Read on to find answers to common sourdough problems. But first, a few general rules for sourdough troubleshooting:

— Don't blame yourself. Reports of the death of your starter are almost certainly exaggerated but you won't fix it with self-criticism or defeatism. So assume the best and start working through the causes and remedies.

— Remember that sourdough yeasts and bacteria are remarkably resilient. Unless you've heated them above 60°C/140°F or doused them with salt (or, heaven forbid, an anti-bacterial 'sanitiser'), they'll be just fine.

— What these micro-organisms need is warmth, water and a source of energy (fuel, if you will), and conditions in which the acid-alkali balance is appropriate to their stage of growth or activity. Fresh flour is the form of fuel most available in bread dough, and getting the acid balance right requires nothing more than a good 'refreshment' every now and then (as described in earlier chapters).

— That said, elaborate 'feeding' regimes are best avoided, not because they will harm a sourdough, but because a) they may waste your time and b) they may make you *think* that you are doing something essential when you aren't.

If your particular problem doesn't exactly match any of the Questions and Answers below, take a closer look: almost all boil down to one issue – how to achieve the optimum balance of yeast and bacterial activity in a natural fermentation.

Q1.
My starter smells odd and there's some liquid on the surface. Is this normal? What should a starter look like?

The short answer is: it depends what stage it's at. Suspend judgement on the smell for a moment, as it's something you'll get used to. The liquid is quite normal – at a certain point in the cycle. That cycle, as we've seen in earlier chapters, is:

- Stage 1: **Starter**
- Stage 2: **Production sourdough**
- Stage 3: **Final dough**

A 'normal' dough changes its appearance as it develops. The flour it is made with makes a difference too. So here is what to look for:

Starter

If this hasn't been refreshed for a while, it will look inactive (few if any bubbles) and some grey-brown liquid may have risen to the surface. The longer it is kept without refreshment (which can be days, weeks or months in the fridge), the more likely it is to have a liquid layer and to smell vinegary.

Production sourdough

This is Stage 2 when you add a small amount of old starter to a larger amount of fresh flour and water, in the process known as *refreshment*. **Rye** starters are almost always made very wet and sloppy; **wheat** starters can be made semi-liquid but are usually more like a normal dough.

Rye doughs: Over 12 to 24 hours, the sourdough will expand as the yeasts produce the gas which makes the surface bubble. Eventually the frothing subsides, sometimes leaving a watery film on the surface. This is a sign that enough acid has accumulated to inhibit further yeast action (until the production sourdough is used to make a final dough).

Wheat doughs: These can be made very runny but are usually almost as firm as an ordinary dough. In about four hours, a wheat production sourdough should double in volume. If left for a long time (unless kept very cool) it may collapse and start smelling strongly acidic.

In short, judge a sourdough on its age and position in the baking process. Even if it looks totally inactive, it is almost certainly not 'dead'. If there are signs of mould, it may still not be terminal – as the next question reveals.

Q2.
My sourdough starter has got some black mould on it. Should I throw it away?

Sourdoughs are set up by nature to be safe and healthy by default, providing simple good practice is followed. However, in the first day or two of a starter's life, when the lactic acid bacteria (LAB) are still 'finding their feet' and have not produced sufficient selective anti-bacterial and anti-fungal compounds to sterilise the mixture, it is possible for moulds to get a foothold, usually as a result of some cross-contamination (a waft or splash of something else in the kitchen) or something lurking in the flour you are using.

In an older starter that is being kept in a tub (perhaps with an incomplete seal), moulds sometimes creep in where there is a lot of 'headspace' above the starter itself. This space contains enough oxygen for any opportunistic moulds that may settle on the sides of the tub or even on the surface of the sourdough to multiply. By contrast, the main bulk of starter is usually sufficiently acid to inhibit any such growth.

Black moulds are unusual and are likely to come from 'dirty' flour or over-relaxed kitchen hygiene. White moulds are more common. Indeed, yeasts and moulds are biologically pretty similar and it is sometimes hard to distinguish between a white mould and the natural efflorescence of yeasts on the surface of an active sourdough starter.

With black moulds, caution is advisable. If black mould has spread over a good part of the surface, it is best to throw the starter away, clean the tub well and begin again. If there is just the odd spot, remove it carefully, stir up the sourdough (with a clean spoon) and give it a 'mini-refreshment' by adding some fresh flour and water. If the black spots reappear, it would be best to start again – perhaps with a different source of flour.

With white moulds, either simply stir the moulds into the body of the mix and, if necessary, transfer to a smaller tub with less space between starter and lid, or skim off the majority of the mould before proceeding in the same manner.

In either case, a couple of refreshments with fresh flour should allow the good microbes to re-establish themselves in your sourdough eco-system.

Q3.
What happens if I haven't got anywhere warm to begin my starter?

Temperature has a big influence on the speed at which yeasts and bacteria ferment. You should try to keep your starter warm during the four-day initial build-up stage because it gets going better. It will work at cooler temperatures, only more slowly. Sometimes novice bakers can mistake this slowness for inactivity – or they just get bored waiting for something to happen. If you don't have an airing cupboard (which is ideal), a good sourdough incubator can be improvised from a cheap plant propagator or an electric heat mat in some sort of insulated box. Direct contact with the heat mat may 'cook' (and therefore kill) some or all of your starter, so place it on a piece of wood or cork tile.

I refreshed my starter according to the instructions, so why didn't my loaf rise?

If your production sourdough (PS) seems inactive and/or your final dough did not rise very much, this could be caused by:

— **Excess acidity, inhibiting the yeasts.** Remedy: make a fresh PS using only half the prescribed percentage of starter (e.g. 25g of [rye] starter, 150g of rye flour and 300g of water). This will dilute the acids in the starter and bring in more new wild yeasts with the fresh flour.

— **Insufficient water.** If your sourdough is too stiff it can take a very long time to ferment. In fact, this is one way of conserving a sourdough for storage or travel, i.e. make it very stiff.

— **Contamination with a 'biocide'**, e.g. heavily chlorinated water, residues of fungicides in non-organic flour, residues of washing-up liquid, salt, etc. This is worth mentioning, though unlikely. Try making the next PS with water that has stood in an open bowl for 24 hours (to let the chlorine evaporate). And always use organic flour, especially wholemeal, because any chemical residues are disproportionately found on the outer bran layers of grain.

If you are sure that you have a vigorous PS, the problem must be occurring in the final dough. Logical trouble-shooting possibilities include:

— **Is there too much salt?** This is by far the commonest problem in bread-making (other than no salt at all), caused by inaccurate scales, misreading of decimal points, etc.

— **Too little liquid** – see above – making the dough too stiff to move.

— **Some other contamination** (unlikely).

— **Proving temperatures so low** that fermentation times are greatly extended (remember, every 5°C drop in temperature doubles the fermentation time).

— **Proving temperatures so high** (over 40°C) that yeasts suffer; again, unlikely, but sometimes people start their breads off on a hot surface (like the back of a range cooker) which is much hotter than 40°C and can locally stress the yeasts.

As to texture, if you are not familiar with 100 per cent rye breads, they can seem very sticky and chewy. Rye holds on to much more water than wheat, so it will always seem 'heavier' than refined white wheat bread. The texture improves with keeping, so try not to cut your rye bread until at least 24 hours after baking. Slice it thinly and it will eat better and go further.

Q5.
Can I use a rye starter to make a wheat loaf?

No problem. This is covered in Chapter 4 (see pp. 63–66). You refresh your rye starter with wheat flour to make a production sourdough that is mostly wheat. If you then use only wheat flour in the final dough, you'll have a wheat sourdough bread with just a hint of rye flavour.

Q6.
My starter smells of pear drops/nail varnish remover/paint stripper. Is it safe to use?

This is a fairly common occurrence with wheat starters, especially in summer: they start smelling of 'pear drops', i.e. a bit chemical. The smell is actually acetone. Under certain conditions, the lactic acid bacteria in the sourdough produce copious amounts of acetic acid, which gives the familiar vinegar smell. Another couple of chemical steps and this can turn into acetone. It can be a bit alarming to sniff your sourdough and get the aroma of nail varnish remover, but it is nothing to worry about. As soon as you dilute the sourdough by refreshing it with flour and water, the smell goes.

Q7.
I'm making a big batch of sourdough bread. Do I need to alter the proportions of production sourdough to final dough?

If you want to make a lot more bread than usual one day and don't have enough starter in the fridge, you can do a little 'intermediate' refreshment to bulk up your starter. If you like precision, you can do the maths and work out exactly how much starter you need to refresh to arrive at the right amount for your purpose.

When scaling up traditional *yeasted* bread doughs, it is logical to reduce the proportion of added baker's yeast because larger doughs hold their heat better than small ones. But where the production sourdough (PS) is the leavening agent of the main dough, this logic doesn't apply, because there are far fewer active yeast cells at work here, and these are slow-acting, naturally occurring yeasts, not laboratory-grown (and sometimes genetically modified) cultures designed for speed. The yeasts in a natural (sourdough) fermentation will, like any yeast, work more slowly at lower temperatures. But because they are fewer in number (by orders of magnitude) than the yeasts added from a highly concentrated source (i.e. a packet), the speed difference when the dough gets a bit warmer is fairly modest.

There is therefore no need to vary the proportion of PS as you scale up your doughs. But remember that the dough temperature will determine rising time more than anything.

This isn't to say, however, that all recipes have to have the same percentage of PS – far from it. In fact, the proportion of production leaven or sourdough in the final dough can be varied considerably with only modest effects on the character of the bread. But here is an interesting paradox.

You'd have thought that the more PS in your final dough, the sourer the bread would be. But the opposite appears to be true, certainly if your final dough has around 60 per cent PS in it as opposed to the more normal 30 per cent or thereabouts. The reason appears to be this: it is the lactic acid bacteria (LAB) that produce the acids that create the sour flavour. LAB work more slowly than yeasts. More PS means more yeasts available to raise the rest of the dough. The dough is therefore ready for the oven a bit sooner, and before the LAB have had time to produce as much acid as they would have over a longer period. Result: *milder-flavoured* bread.

Q8.
Can I use a wheat starter to make a spelt sourdough?

Yes, you can use the wheat sourdough (starter) to make a spelt sourdough. Just use spelt flour when you refresh the sourdough (i.e. make a production sourdough) and after two refreshments you will have an almost wholly spelt leaven. A word of caution, though: spelt flour ferments more quickly than wheat, so you may need to lower the temperature and reduce the refreshment time of your spelt production sourdoughs.

Remember, too, that if you use up all your wheat starter in making a spelt sourdough, the bit of your production sourdough that you keep back will be mostly spelt. If you want to maintain a pure wheat starter, you should refresh it only with wheat flour. The same applies to rye-wheat hybrid starters (see Q5).

Q9.
Why does my plain rye bread sometimes get a hole under the crust and how can I prevent this?

The problem isn't confined to rye breads or even sourdoughs in general, but the answers below are mostly relevant to these breads. Here is a list of possible factors:

— **The dough is too wet** – weak rye gluten is unable to hold the gas-filled structure together at the most vulnerable part of the loaf, i.e. the top.
  Remedy: reduce the water in the final dough.

— **Overactive production sourdough.**
  Remedy: shorten the production sourdough fermentation time and/or reduce the proportion of production sourdough in the final dough.

- **Over-proof** (rising too long and/or too much dough in the tin). The structure begins to bubble and collapse at the top and falls away from under the top crust, which forms a 'bridge' that may look OK but hides a crumbly centre.

- **Under-proof** (not being left long enough to rise in the tin). Sounds paradoxical in view of the over-proof comments above, but an under-proved loaf will try to expand in the oven and, if it is unable to break through the crust, may produce a distorted internal structure.

- **Skinning of the dough during proof.** If the dough surface has dried out during proving it cannot expand as much as it wants and the gas bubbles immediately under the top crust will rupture and subsequently collapse. **Remedy:** prove in a warm, humid atmosphere, e.g. a polythene bag that is inflated to stop it collapsing onto the dough.

- **Trapped water.** If you trap water in the middle of the dough during moulding with wet hands, it is possible that this will 'blow up' into a hole as the trapped water vaporises during baking. (However, the chances of this always occurring just under the crust are small.)

- **Tin too wide.** Rye gluten (yes, it does have some, but not the stretchy type like wheat) is not very strong, and it can't easily support the structure of dough in a wide tin. Many tins sold in kitchen shops are a bit low and wide for rye bread. See Resources (p. 154) for places to get better-shaped baking tins.

Can I make sourdough bread in the great outdoors?

Yes, it's actually the perfect bread to make on a camping trip, for example. This is what you'll need:

— **Sourdough starter** (active, i.e. used before and known to work)
— **Flour** (whatever is to hand)
— **Salt** (can be derived entirely from a 50/50 mix of fresh and sea water, assuming sea water is 3.5 per cent salt)
— **Clean water** (suggest using bottled water)
— **Bowl** for mixing
— **Bonfire/firepit/camping stove**
— **Flat stone or cast-iron pot with lid** ('Dutch oven')

To keep things as simple as possible, use the all-in-one method described on p. 79 ('Overnight No-knead Sourdough').

Mix the flour, salt, water and sourdough starter together in the bowl. Knead briefly, cover and leave for 18 hours plus. Keep out of cooling draughts and direct sun. Don't leave inside a tent on a sunny day as it will get too hot.

Prepare your bonfire or fire pit well in advance, so that you have a pile of glowing embers, rather than a roaring fire, ready for the risen dough. The latter can be tipped onto a stone that has been heated in the embers for at least an hour (preferably longer). Or it can simply be turned onto a bed of ash and covered with ash and embers. In this case, the baked loaf will be encrusted with ash and small bits of charcoal, but this can be brushed or scraped off (as you would if eating potatoes done the same way).

The 'Dutch oven' method is the easiest (but you won't want to carry one with you if you are backpacking). Pre-heat a cast-iron pot on or in the fire; tip the risen dough gently into it, replace the lid and rake embers up around the pot.

Baking time will depend on the method used, but note that the intensity and direct conduction of heat from a wood fire may cook the bread surprisingly quickly, usually in around 20 minutes.

Q11.
What is the best sourdough bread for children?

The two commonest complaints from children encountering sourdough bread for the first time are its flavour and the hardness of its crust. This is not surprising, given the mild flavour and soft texture of most shop-bought breads.

Sour flavour can be kept to a minimum by increasing the proportion of production sourdough to final dough (see Q7) and by keeping the dough warm and wet, so that it rises relatively quickly.

Hard crusts can be softened by dusting the dough heavily in flour before its final proof: the flour layer interferes with the formation of a crisp crust in the early stages of baking. Another trick is to wrap the just-baked loaf in a cotton cloth so that it sweats a little: the crust will absorb the moisture and go soft.

The most 'accessible' breads for children are soft, light recipes such as ciabatta (p. 105). In the latter case, a good slosh of olive oil after baking keeps the crust soft. And there is always pizza, of course (p. 110): the vegetable and cheese topping is always moist and tasty and although the bottom crust is anything but flabby (if baked properly), tender gums usually seem able to tackle it in this form.

Q12.
Why do you often use a combination of white and wholemeal flours? Are there right and wrong flours to use for sourdough baking?

Choosing flour for sourdough bread-making means balancing nutritional quality, biological activity, flavour and elasticity. White flour delivers the latter, but is deficient in the first three qualities. The outer layers of wheat (and rye, barley, etc.) grain are composed of the bran and germ that harbour key minerals and vitamins. They are also where the natural yeasts and bacteria, so vital to the functioning of a good sourdough, are to be found. The flavour of pure white flour is mild, too, so it follows that flour with at least some of the outer grain layers mixed into it is better on all four counts.

However, not everyone wants to make bread with straight wholemeal/wholewheat flour all the time. What is often missing in the market place is a light flour which, while having less coarse bran particles than wholemeal, nevertheless has the wheatgerm (and its vital vitamin E) intact and enough fine bran to give a pleasant flavour, good biological activity and reasonable digestive properties. Such flour, if available, often goes under names such as 'wheatmeal', 'farmhouse', or '85% extraction', the latter referring to the percentage of the whole grain left in the flour.

If you see this sort of flour, it is well worth trying some. But if you can't get hold of any, or don't want a proliferation of flour bags in your store cupboard, mixing white and wholemeal may be the answer.

There is an even better way to vary the type of flour you use for different purposes. All you need is a supply of stoneground wholemeal/wholewheat flour and a sieve or set of sieves. Stoneground flour, unlike roller-milled flour, will have all the germ oil evenly dispersed through it. So, if you pass it through a fine sieve to get something close to white flour, you will remove most of the bran but not all of the germ oil and its vitamin E. Don't throw away the bran siftings. They make a good dusting flour for dough proved in baskets and can be fermented for a day with some sourdough starter for a very nutritious addition to a light loaf. Or they can be added back to the flour in varying proportions to get just the quality you want.

While there are no absolute rights and wrongs about flour choice, two points are worth bearing in mind. First, it makes no sense to spend extra money on buying highly refined 'speciality' flour such as Italian '00' ('double zero') which is even more devoid of nutrients than standard white flour. It contributes no flavour and little biological vitality to sourdough breads. Second, the prevalence (according to official tests) in non-organic flour of residues of pesticides and herbicides whose sole function is to destroy biological activity makes buying organic the best choice.

Once you've got the hang of it, baking with sourdough is tremendously liberating. That starter in your fridge is a powerhouse of possibilities. It requires nothing more of us than that we appreciate its basic needs and *use* it – to make bread with our own hands, in our own time.

Sourdough is much more than a yeast substitute or a trendier way of baking by numbers. It only works if we understand and respect the life inside. It challenges us to be patient, observant and creative.

It should come as no surprise, then, that almost every kind of bread can be made with sourdough. This chapter reveals sourdough's flexibility, by showing that not everything made with natural fermentation need be bold, craggy and – perish the thought – ever so slightly macho. Let us celebrate some softer, flatter, sweeter breads by discovering sourdough's sensitive side.

———————

Sourdough ciabatta and soft rolls

Makes 3 medium-sized ciabatta and 12 soft rolls

A popular Italian bread-making tradition uses an overnight yeasted sponge known as a *biga* (see p. 14). This contains almost all the flour in the recipe, a small amount of baker's yeast and not much water, making it a stiff – and therefore slow-rising – dough. The recipe that follows uses the same idea but with a sourdough starter in place of the baker's yeast. Note how little starter is required – less than 5 per cent of the weight of the production sourdough. The resulting dough can be baked in the familiar slipper shape or as floury rolls, batched together.

Ciabatta is just one version of a very loose, usually entirely white, dough that appears in various guises in Italy's distinctively regional cuisine. All share the very open texture and chewy crumb that are telltale signs of dough made with a high water content. Flour or olive oil are often used to stop a thick crust forming, making for a generally soft eat.

This dough makes a good soft roll, too, if shaped conventionally and floured well to keep it soft.

Ciabatta production sourdough

Ingredients	Weight	
	grams	oz
Wheat sourdough starter	85	3
White flour	910	32
Wholemeal flour	230	8
Water (30°C/86°F)	625	22
Total	**1850**	**65**

Note: 1 millilitre of water weighs 1 gram

Method

Tip: Use tepid water in winter, but keep it cooler in summer.

Dissolve your sourdough starter in the water (always a good plan with such a small amount of starter, as it ensures that it is evenly spread throughout the dough). Mix the flours in and knead the resulting fairly stiff dough for a couple of minutes until it is fairly smooth. Cover with a lid or polythene bag and leave to ferment for 14 to 18 hours.

Ciabatta final dough

Ingredients	Weight	
	grams	oz
Refreshed ciabatta production sourdough	1700	60
White flour	100	3.5
'Farmhouse' (i.e. sifted wholemeal) flour*	35	1.25
Olive oil	40	1.5
Sea salt	15	0.5
Water (30°C/86°F)	250	9
Total	**2140**	**76**

Note: 1 millilitre of water weighs 1 gram

* This is optional, but gives a nuttier flavour than white flour alone

Method

There will be a little production sourdough left over after you have weighed out the 1700g. Put this back in your wheat sourdough pot in the fridge.

Work the fresh flours, oil, salt and water into the production sourdough. The dough should become quite loose and stretchy after a few minutes of kneading, preferably with wet hands, on a wet worktop. Adjust the water content, if necessary, to achieve a very soft dough.

If this is anything like the consistency of the doughs you normally put in a tin, it is probably too dry.

When the dough shows a slightly shiny surface, with well-developed gluten (i.e. slightly springy) and considerable extensibility (it can be gently stretched quite a long way without breaking), stop kneading. Rest the dough for a few minutes.

Divide it into the requisite portions – 300g for ciabatta, 100g for rolls.

Finishing the ciabatta

Using floury hands and a generous flick of flour on the table, divide the dough into pieces. Lay these on the floury surface and rest them for a few more minutes to ensure that the gluten is fully relaxed.

Trying to avoid working raw flour into the middle of the dough piece, roll it up like a Swiss roll, once or twice folding the ends towards the middle as you go. Finish what should be a reasonably tight sausage-shaped loaf with the 'seam' hidden underneath. Roll this whole baton in flour and place it on a baking tray, preferably lined with silicone paper (baking parchment) or matting. Keep your

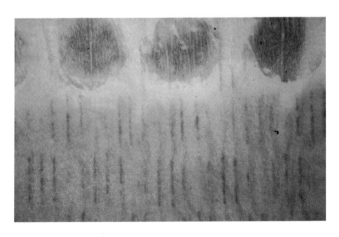

ciabatta pieces a good 10cm (4in) apart because they will flow outwards during proving and baking and you want to allow the oven's heat to form an all-round crust as soon as possible.

Proof time can be as much as five hours for these breads, but will probably be less, particularly in warm weather. Since the dough is (or should be) soft and mobile, it will expand considerably in the oven, so a degree of under-proof is permissible.

If you have a pizza stone or similar, use it for this bread because direct bottom heat will give the ciabatta better lift and a more tubular shape.

Finishing the soft rolls

Divide the rolls in the same way as the larger ciabatta pieces, placing them on a floured surface. Dusting flour like talcum powder on your hands, pick up a piece of dough in each, work it around between your hand and the bench until its surface is covered with just enough flour to stop it sticking. Try to avoid rolling a lot of raw flour into the middle of the dough.

Using a circular motion of your hands (rotating in opposite directions), press the dough down under your palms until it pulls together and tries to stick to the table. Gradually release the downward pressure as you cup your hands, keeping your finger tips on the table all the time. The dough should form a tight ball with all the tucks and cracks hidden underneath. If the dough just skids about and doesn't 'come together', there is too much flour on the worktop. If the dough sticks, scrape it off and dust the worktop lightly before trying again.

Dip these rolls immediately in a bowl of flour, flipping them over to make sure that they are completely covered. This layer of flour acts a bit like a heat shield, protecting the surface of the dough during baking and delaying the formation of a hard crust.

Place the rolls about 2.5cm (1in) apart on a lightly floured baking tray. Prove (under a loose cover) until the dough pieces are just touching. This is called 'batching', where the individual rolls or loaves fuse together during baking. It makes economical use of the baking surface and reduces the overall proportion of crust, making for a softer eat.

Baking

Both ciabatta and rolls should be baked in a hot oven (230°C/445°F) for 8 to 12 minutes. The distance between crust and core is not great, so they should bake through more quickly than large loaves baked in tins. The more quickly a loaf is baked, the more moisture it retains inside and the moister and more delicious its eating quality will be. It may keep a little longer, too.

Soft sourdough rolls

Pizza and crisp bread

Makes 3 large or 6 small pizzas and 6 crisp breads

These two may seem very different but they are, when all's said and done, just thin bits of dough. One is covered with vegetables and cheese and is flash-fired to produce a predominantly moist result, while the other is baked to a crunch.

Sourdough has many advantages for both these breads. It ferments slowly, so pizza bases or crisp bread shapes can be prepared hours in advance of baking. In fact they are better like this because, after a long proof, the dough will be 'ripe' in flavour and will stretch out easily.

Using the same basic dough for several different finished products is economical of time and energy, as this recipe demonstrates. Make the dough when you have a moment, divide it up and roll some pieces out as pizza bases. Mix the rest of the dough with whatever spices or seeds you have prepared and divide and roll as described below. Dress the pizza bases with toppings and bake them in a hot oven until the base is brown and firm and the topping bubbling nicely.

Then, when the heat has subsided, put the long-fermented crisp breads in and let them gently dry out. The longer the proof the crisp breads have, the 'shorter' (less chewy) they will be, because the tough gluten protein chains will have been partially weakened by the gentle action over time of sourdough bacteria.

Make these and you'll never want a potato crisp or an extruded chemically-leavened cracker again.

Sourdough pizza

Pizza production sourdough

Ingredients	Weight	
	grams	oz
Wheat sourdough starter (old)	180	6
White or 'farmhouse' (i.e. sifted wholemeal) flour	240	8
Water (30°C/86°F)	150	5
Total	**570**	**19**

Note: 1 millilitre of water weighs 1 gram

Method

Mix everything together and ferment for 4 hours at room temperature or longer at lower temperature, depending on your plans.

Pizza final dough

Ingredients	Weight	
	grams	oz
Refreshed pizza production sourdough	425	15
White flour or farmhouse flour or a mixture	450	16
Olive oil	40	1.5
Sea salt	8	0.25
Water (30°C/86°F)	280	10
Total	**1203**	**43**

Note: 1 millilitre of water weighs 1 gram

Method

Make a 'soaker' of the fresh flour, salt and water and leave it to stand for half an hour or so. Add the production sourdough and olive oil and knead for a few minutes on a wet surface. The dough should come together into a smooth and stretchy mass. The surface will change from a slightly lumpy, 'orange peel' effect to something smoother and slightly shiny – a bit like chamois leather.

Rest the dough under cover for a few minutes and then divide it. You'll need roughly the following amount of dough per item:

Large pizza	150g	(5oz)
Small pizza	80g	(3oz)
Crisp bread	120g	(4oz)

Finishing pizzas

Using a light dusting of flour, stretch or roll out the dough until it is about 20–25cm (8–10in) in diameter for the large pieces or 12–15cm (5–6in) for the small ones. This can be quite easily done with a rolling pin but the result is rather lifeless. Try holding the dough up like a cloth and slowly rotating it as your fingers gently grip the edge, allowing gravity to pull the dough downwards. It may end up rather uneven, but this will be compensated by a more lively and open-textured dough. If you've ever felt that the bit of dough under the pizza topping tasted much like thin cardboard, try this method. The dough may get a bit thin in places, but it can be patched over – and any such blemishes will all be hidden under the topping. The overall effect of hand-pulling rather than rolling is a more interesting texture and an authentic artisan appearance.

Incidentally, forget all that 'throwing the dough up in the air' exhibitionism: it's only possible with a dough made with such refined flour and toughened protein that your digestive system will be in a right spin for hours after the meal.

At this point the pizza bases can be set out on a baking tray to prove. Keep them covered with a polythene sheet or damp tea towel in order to prevent the surface drying and cracking. When you're ready, you can either top them with tomato paste, sweated peppers, onions, mushrooms, etc., finishing with thinly sliced or grated cheese (there are tasty alternatives to the default mozzarella, so feel free to experiment), or freeze them for later use. Slip a piece of silicone paper (baking parchment) between each pizza base and put the whole pile in a polythene bag, squeeze out all the air and tie up the end.

These bases will last in the freezer for several months and you can remove them one by one very easily if they are separated by papers. To defrost and use, simply lay a base on a baking tray, place your chosen toppings on and then give it a couple of hours to finish proving. If you can't wait, you can bake them pretty much straight from the freezer, but allow a little longer in the oven. All in all, it is not difficult to have a first-class sourdough pizza ready to bake exactly when it suits you.

Finishing crisp breads

Take a lump of finished dough which has been allowed to relax for a few minutes. This makes working the extra ingredients into it much easier.

You can, of course, make plain crisp breads, in which case simply skip to the rolling-out instructions on p. 114.

The possibilities for adding interesting flavours and textures are infinite. Here are two suggestions:

Black pepper crisp breads

Ingredients	Weight	
	grams	oz
Pizza final dough (see p. 110)	360	13
Black pepper	5	0.2
Total	**365**	**13**

Scale at approx 120g (4.25oz) each to make three large crisp breads

Note: 1 millilitre of water weighs 1 gram

Grate the pepper freshly, if possible. Five grams is plenty for this amount of dough. For a stronger hit, use chilli powder, but go easy – a gram or two (a large pinch or two) will do.

Sesame and mustard crisp breads

Ingredients	Weight	
	grams	oz
Pizza final dough (see p. 110)	360	13
Sesame seeds	40	1.5
Yellow mustard seeds	10	0.3
Total	**410**	**15**

Scale at approx 135g (4.75oz) each to make three large crisp breads

Note: 1 millilitre of water weighs 1 gram

It's best to crush the seeds beforehand, in a mortar or with a rolling pin on the table. This releases their oils and helps spread their flavours through the dough. Sprinkle the crushed seed onto the dough and work it in the same way as described for the black pepper dough above.

Rolling out

Divide the prepared dough into pieces as indicated on p. 113.

Dusting the worktop lightly with flour, roll each piece out with a rolling pin into a shape roughly 30cm (12in) long by 7.5cm (3in) wide. The dough may shrink back as you are rolling it out, but half a minute's rest will relax the gluten and allow the dough to be elongated without tearing. Evenness is important at this stage because any very thin patches will burn during baking.

Set the long 'tongues' out on a baking tray, dusted with a little flour. Dock (i.e. prick) them with a fork firmly so that the holes go right through the dough. This is to stop the dough puffing up like pitta bread during baking.

Prove for as long as you like (up to 5 hours is fine). Have your oven at a steady 170°C/340°F. You can bake these breads at a higher temperature but the risk of burning is greater. Just before you bake, get your fingers under the strips of dough and spread them a little further longways, aiming to leave them slightly uneven. The idea is to help the crisp breads to twist and distort a little during baking.

Bake for as long as is necessary to dry the crisp breads out completely. Check after 15 minutes, but go on as long as the dough is not colouring up too much. It's no crime to return them to the oven for a while if they go a bit limp as they cool down.

Store the cooled crisp breads in an airtight tin or a well-sealed polythene bag. They will last for ages, if you let them.

Sesame & mustard crispbread

Sourdough crumpets

Sourdough crumpets

Makes 8 crumpets

Soft, alluring (especially when hot), indulgent ... we all seem to love crumpets. If not exactly available on demand, sourdough crumpets are much easier than yeasted ones to slot into a busy schedule. Slower fermentation means a bigger 'window' to get them baked.

Crumpet dough is the ultimate wet dough. It is pourable. This makes it, as we've seen, the ideal medium for sourdough yeasts to express their *joie de vivre* in the form of bubbles of carbon dioxide gas. While they are doing this in their decorous way over several hours, the lactic acid bacteria have time to give what is otherwise a bland dough some real flavour. Better still, the bacteria start to soften the tough wheat proteins that make crumpets altogether too rubbery when made with fast-acting yeast.

Crumpet production sourdough

Ingredients	Weight	
	grams	oz
Rye (or wheat) sourdough starter (old)	80	3
White flour	70	2.5
Wholemeal/wholewheat flour	30	1
Water (35°C/95°F)	60	2
Total	**240**	**9**

Note: 1 millilitre of water weighs 1 gram

Mix all together and ferment for 12 to 16 hours.

Crumpet final dough

Ingredients	Weight	
	grams	oz
Refreshed crumpet production sourdough (from previous page)	210	7.5
White flour	125	4.5
Wholemeal/wholewheat flour	65	2.25
Olive oil	10	0.3
Sea salt	5	0.2
Water (35°C/95°F)	235	8.25
Total	**650**	**23**

Note: 1 millilitre of water weighs 1 gram

Method

Mix everything together using fairly warm water. The oil helps to soften the dough slightly. The mixture should be very loose, almost liquid.

Cover and ferment until the whole mixture is bubbling and has risen appreciably. If you use a transparent bowl or tub you will be able to see the very open texture of the dough through the sides. It could take 4 to 8 hours for this process, depending on the temperature of water used and conditions in your kitchen.

It is ready to use when it has bubbled up quite considerably, but it will work fine long after this point is reached. If you leave it a very long time, your crumpets will taste stronger and, for some people, too sour. If you use the mixture too soon, the crumpets will be dense.

Depositing the sourdough crumpets

To bake crumpets

Prepare a frying pan or hot plate on a gas or electric hob. Heat up until quite hot, but not so hot that a thin layer of oil brushed over the surface turns immediately to smoke.

Use whatever muffin rings you have available. Plain cookie cutters will do. The recipe above produces about eight in rings that measure 85mm (3.5in) in diameter by 30mm (1.25in) high. Non-stick ones make life easier.

Grease or oil a ring and place it on the hot plate which has been brushed with a little oil. Using a soup ladle, pour about 80g (3oz) of the bubbling dough into the ring. It should come just over halfway up the side of the ring. After a few minutes, the wet top of the mixture will begin to solidify with a kind of honeycomb appearance. As soon as the top is completely firm, remove the ring and flip the crumpet over to complete baking. It is done when both top and bottom are nicely browned and the sides, when squeezed, spring back and do not feel soggy.

The time taken to cook the crumpets through will depend a bit on local conditions (the thickness of your frying pan, for example) and on how many crumpets you make at once. This is a very wet mixture, so don't expect it to bake quickly; 20 to 25 minutes to do both sides is quite possible.

To serve in the traditional way, toast the crumpet on an open fire on the end of a long fork, then split (don't cut) round the 'waist' to reveal a torn dough, with shiny caverns into which butter will obligingly melt. A toaster does the job perfectly well, too.

Once you've enjoyed the flavour of a sourdough crumpet, the yeasted (or, worse still, chemically raised) ones will seem dull by comparison.

Sweet sourdough

Sourdough, being simply a natural fermentation, is quite capable of raising sweet breads as well as savoury ones. Indeed, since at least the 1970s a curious version of sweet sourdough has been doing the rounds in the form of the 'friendship cake'. A recent manifestation has gone by names such as 'Hermann' or 'Hermione'. The recipe seems to have evolved from a branch of alchemy and owes little to modern fermentation science. It is powered by genial goodwill and lots of smiles, which is no bad thing, but it places little trust in the sourdough principle, since users are often told to use extra baker's yeast (and even baking soda) to support whatever natural yeasts are supposed to be present.

This points to the main 'problem' of making sweet sourdough: sugar. Small amounts of added sugar (i.e. not the sugars converted by enzymes from wheat starches) can act as a yeast 'food', which is why old-fashioned recipes often suggest starting a yeasty ferment with a little sugar to help things along. But once the sugar concentration reaches a certain point (around a 10 per cent solution), yeast activity is inhibited. So the sweeter the dough, the weaker the yeast activity and the slower the rise.

Sourdough yeasts may fare a bit better than baker's yeast in sweet doughs, despite being fewer in number, because of their ability to metabolise maltose sugars at slightly higher concentrations, but there's no getting away from the fact that sweet doughs either need lots of extra yeast or plenty of time. Sourdough naturally works with the latter and so doesn't need the former.

Honey and ginger sourdough bannock

Honey and ginger sourdough bannock

Makes two 750g (26oz) bannocks

Based very loosely on the traditional Selkirk bannock
from the Scottish Borders, this is a fruity bread enriched
with butter and a little honey. The fennel seeds in the fruit
soaker give an aniseed twist.

Fruit mix

Ingredients	Weight	
	grams	oz
Sultanas	130	4.5
Raisins	130	4.5
Ginger (crystallised)	120	4.25
Ginger (powdered)	10	0.3
Fennel seeds	20	0.7
Orange juice	90	3
Total	**500**	**17**

Note: 1 millilitre of water weighs 1 gram

Put everything into a polythene bag, shake it well to mix
all the ingredients, seal and leave to soak for at least a
day, giving the bag a quick swoosh whenever the spirit
moves you.

Bannock production sourdough

Ingredients	Weight	
	grams	oz
Wheat sourdough starter (old)	110	4
White flour	110	4
Wholemeal/wholewheat flour	35	1
Water (dependent on intended timing)	110	4
Total	**365**	**13**

Note: 1 millilitre of water weighs 1 gram

Mix and ferment for 4 hours at room temperature or 12 to 16 hours at 10°C/50°F. Use warm water for a short refreshment, cooler for longer.

Bannock final dough

Ingredients	Weight	
	grams	oz
Refreshed production sourdough (from above)	275	10
White flour	200	7
Wholemeal/wholewheat flour	200	7
Butter	60	2
Honey	30	1
Sea salt	5	0.2
Water (35°C/95°F)	230	8
Total	**1000**	**35**

Note: 1 millilitre of water weighs 1 gram

Method

Make a soaker with the flour, salt, honey and water. Cover and leave for half an hour. Knead for a minute or two on a wet surface, then work in the butter. Once the dough is 'cleared' and there are no lumps of butter left, add the production sourdough and knead for a few more minutes until the dough is soft and pliable.

Rest the dough for a few minutes. Flatten it out on the table and spread the soaked fruit mix over it. Roll the dough up, turn the 'sausage' through 90 degrees, flatten it a bit and roll it up again, thus spreading the fruit fairly evenly through the dough.

Divide into two pieces, shape each one, dip in flour (preferably brown rice flour) and place in a prepared round proving basket. Cover loosely and prove in a warm place out of draughts for 4 to 6 hours.

Tip out onto a baking tray or stone and bake in a moderate oven (180°C/355°F) for 35 to 45 minutes.

Optional: immediately after removing from the oven, glaze generously with a mixture that is two parts honey, one part cream (pouring or whipping). To glaze both loaves you will need about 100g (3.5oz) honey and 50g (1.75oz) cream. Warm the honey so that it is runny, then stir in the cream. Brush this mixture onto the loaves when they are hot so that the glaze soaks in. A second coat will leave a glossy, sticky finish.

7

**Waste Not,
Want Not:
The seven
days of bread**

A shocking fact was revealed by government-sponsored research quite recently: upwards of 30 per cent of UK bread is thrown away uneaten, much of it still in its wrapper.

Whatever this sad statistic tells us about the connection between low price and low esteem in industrial baking, part of the problem may stem from skewed perceptions of freshness and a cultural aversion to ageing. Almost all industrial loaves are laced with synthetic enzymes to keep them soft for days or weeks. If every slice is identically 'fresh', the only way of divining its real age is by consulting the 'use by' label. Thus trust in our own sensory experience is undermined by the dictatorship of dates and an irrational fear of putrefaction.

In contrast, the sourdough baker embraces the passing of time as an indispensable contributor to the quality of, and our delight in, bread.

Without time, sourdough fermentation has no meaning. And I would argue that our pleasure in baked bread is one-dimensional (if not illusory) if it excludes *any* part of a loaf's passage from newly baked to stale.

Even sourdough starters, which have a habit of accumulating and threatening to outgrow their containers, are far from a 'waste' product. So never throw any surplus away, but use it (no matter how old and sour) in small quantities – up to 10 per cent – in almost any yeasted bread, where acid by-products will both flavour and strengthen the dough, and very likely keep it moister for longer.

It's all a matter of definition. If we get the bread right, it simply cannot be wasted, because it is useful and enjoyable throughout its life. And what could be more relevant to modern lives? If we're really too busy to bake and rushing to the shops isn't an option, let's make the best of what's left.

Here, as a celebration of time's benign role in sourdough baking, I propose 'The Seven Days of Bread'. See how the gradual mellowing of a baked loaf suggests a week of different and delicious uses.

The loaf we used for the photo-montage that follows was a simple sourdough wheat bread, made to the recipe on pp. 42–56 in Chapter 3. But it doesn't much matter which loaf you choose, because the principles hold for all real bread.

As soon as it is baked and cooled, the process of 'staling' begins. Slowly, the starches harden and the moist crumb dries out. In sourdough breads, the flavour becomes more pronounced and 'mature'. With each change comes a new adaptation to what the bread can offer.

These, of course, are mere suggestions – and fairly obvious ones at that. I'm sure you will come up with more and better ideas.

The Seven Days of Bread

—

DAY 1

Fresh

—

Just out of the oven.
No butter (but some
self-control) needed.
Perfect.

DAY 2
Sandwich

—

Still soft, but firm enough to hold a filling.

DAY 3
Toast

—

Drying out. Toasting both crisps the outside of the bread and softens the starches of the inner layer of the slice (unless you go on too long). Best eaten just warm, not hot.

DAY 4
Bruschetta
—

Getting quite dry, but not 'stale'. Toast lightly, top with peppers, onions, olives, goats' cheese, etc., and finish under the grill.

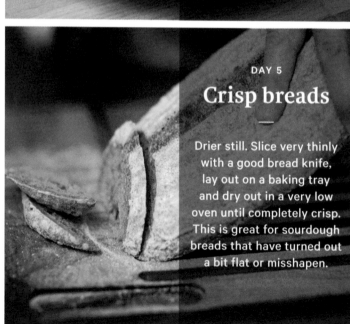

DAY 5
Crisp breads
—

Drier still. Slice very thinly with a good bread knife, lay out on a baking tray and dry out in a very low oven until completely crisp. This is great for sourdough breads that have turned out a bit flat or misshapen.

DAY 6
Croutons
—

Hard tack. Slice into 1.5cm (0.5in) cubes, fry in a little olive oil (they'll try to soak up a lot) until they are taking a little colour. Cool, bag up and use later, or simply toss into a green salad.

DAY 7
Breadcrumbs
—

Probably beginning to crack a little as the interior dries and shrinks. Grate, either by hand on a coarse cheese grater or in a food processor. Bag and freeze. Or stir a little olive oil through the crumbs with your fingers, and use to top a vegetable casserole.

8

In Your Own Time:
From commuter bakes
to overnight success

The sourdough baking process requires many hours, but not of *your* time. This final chapter shows how easy it is to fit sourdough baking into busy lifestyles, with suggested schedules for slotting the vital fermentation time into periods when you are asleep, at work or otherwise occupied. The 'tolerance' of sourdough (compared to fast-acting yeasted dough) is one of its greatest advantages, especially when you can't spend all day in the kitchen. Sourdough works slowly, so the chances of missing some narrow 'window' for performing a vital task are minimised.

Using a classic sourdough rye bread as our chief example, we'll see how the same basic bread can be produced over different timescales by varying temperature, water content, or sourdough concentration.

These principles apply to all the different types of sourdough bread we've covered, so don't worry if rye bread isn't your favourite.

Russian sourdough rye bread

Makes one large or two small loaves

The recipe below is based on the 'black' bread that I survived on as a student in Moscow in the 1960s. It isn't really black, by the way, unless your oven's out of control. The crumb is more of a grey colour. It's moist, chewy, satisfying, and deliciously sour.

The ingredients couldn't be simpler:

Rye sourdough starter
Rye flour (wholemeal ['dark rye'] in the main)
Sea salt
Bread tin(s)
Water

Testing the consistency of rye sourdough

Process

As we've seen, there are five steps in the sequence from starter to baked rye bread:

1. **Make production sourdough**
2. **Ferment**
3. **Make final dough**
4. **Prove**
5. **Bake**

These are typical durations for each stage:

Action	Duration	Active time
	hh:mm	mins
Make production sourdough	00:10	10
Ferment production sourdough	16:00	
Weigh out and mix final dough	00:15	15
Prove	03:00	
Bake	00:40	
Remove from oven; tidy up	00:10	10
Total elapsed time/active time	**20:15**	**35**

Rye dough requires very little kneading, so just half an hour's work in three short bursts over a total of about 20 hours is all that it takes. We'll look at some real-world timings shortly. First, the rye starter must be refreshed to make a production sourdough to build up the yeast and bacterial population. Rye flour in its natural state is sticky and it *must* be fermented with sourdough. If the sourdough isn't mature enough, the end product will have a claggy crumb that's impossible to cut.

Rye production sourdough

Ingredients	Weight	
	grams	oz
Rye starter (old)	50	2
Wholemeal (dark) rye flour	150	6
Water (35°C/95°F)	300	12
Total	**500**	**20**

Note: 1 millilitre of water weighs 1 gram

Method

Use hands to stir the starter to disperse any liquid on the top and bring up any sludge from the bottom of the tub. Mix 50g (2oz) of starter with half the water, which should be fairly warm (35–40°C). Add the flour and mix to a lump-free paste. Add the rest of the water and stir until the mixture is smooth and fairly sloppy – the texture of thin porridge. Cover with a lid or poly bag and leave in a warm place, out of draughts, for about 16 hours.

That is the refreshment completed. Take 440g (15.5oz) of this to make the final dough. Put the remaining 50g (2oz) or so (the maths aren't exact because bits of dough get lost on fingers and bowls) back into your starter pot in the fridge.

Russian sourdough rye bread final dough

Ingredients	Weight	
	grams	oz
Rye production sourdough (from previous page)	440	16
Wholemeal (dark) rye flour (or light or a mixture)	340	12
Sea salt	8	0.25
Water (30°C/86°F – approximately)	180	6.5
Total	**968**	**35**

Note: 1 millilitre of water weighs 1 gram

Method

Put the production sourdough in a mixing bowl first (so there's less chance of dry floury lumps being left in the bottom) and add the rye flour(s), salt and almost all of the water.

Mix it all together with one hand. The gluten in rye doesn't go stretchy, so no kneading is necessary beyond mixing everything thoroughly. Getting the water content right is a little trickier. Essentially, all-rye dough needs to be almost as soft as a cake batter but without the slippery element that added fat brings. Rye flour, especially dark rye which has all the bran intact, soaks up a great deal of water and takes a little while to do so. It is therefore better to err on the side of more water, rather than less. Don't even think about kneading 'on a floury surface': adding flour soon makes a rye dough even stickier.

Of course, it is possible to have too much of a good thing. This rye dough should not be so wet that it is pourable. Have a bowl of water handy, scrape any dough from your hands and moisten them, your scraper and the worktop. Slurp the dough out of the bowl, wetting the scraper as necessary to stop it getting too sticky. Pick up the lump of dough with wet hands, smooth it into a loaf-shaped rectangle and slide it into a prepared tin. With a bit of practice, you can drop it in without touching the sides.

Even if it goes in a bit lopsided, resist the temptation to fiddle. Rye dough is self-levelling and will fill the tin nicely all by itself.

Cover the tin loosely (so the cover won't come into contact with the rising dough) and put it in a reasonably warm, draught-free place to prove. It may take anything from 2 to 5 hours or more, depending on temperature and the vitality of your sourdough. If it doubles in volume, you are doing well. As a dough of this type expands, it splits naturally (no stretchy gluten in rye) and you will notice the top surface beginning to 'craze'. This is as it should be.

When fully risen, rye dough is fragile and needs to be handled gently. Over-proving – or a bump on the way to the oven – can cause collapse and a disappointingly concave top.

Bake at 230°C/445°F for 10 minutes, reducing to 210°C/410°F for another half-hour or so. Traditionally, Russian rye bread has quite a dark top crust. Too low an oven or too short a bake can produce a rather anaemic-looking loaf. If in doubt, leave it a bit longer.

Don't attempt to cut this bread until a day after baking to allow the naturally sticky crumb to firm up a bit. Wrapped in a polythene bag (when cold), it keeps for many days. The texture firms gradually and the flavour deepens.

Time shifts

This bread follows a schedule that allows the fermentation process to play out at normal room temperature, without any attempt to adjust it to fit in with other demands on the baker's time. Even without any change of recipe, these schedules can work in various ways. Here are some suggestions.

1. Early riser

Refresh starter before breakfast, make bread early evening, bake before bedtime.

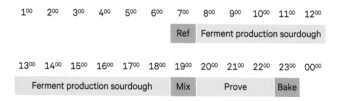

1⁰⁰	2⁰⁰	3⁰⁰	4⁰⁰	5⁰⁰	6⁰⁰	7⁰⁰	8⁰⁰	9⁰⁰	10⁰⁰	11⁰⁰	12⁰⁰

Notes

1. *Ref = refresh* sourdough starter to make a production sourdough.
2. Start and finish times are approximate and will depend on your judgement on the day.
3. Production sourdough fermentation has been reduced to about 12 hours. This is normally ample time but it can be extended a bit by starting earlier or finishing later. Use it as the 'balancing factor' in your schedule.

2. Late developer

Refresh starter last thing, make dough next evening, bake before bedtime.

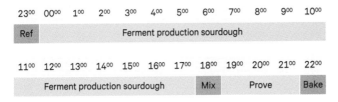

Notes

1. Production sourdough fermentation is up to about 18 hours. Plenty of time for good flavour to develop.

3. Morning off

Refresh starter at lunchtime, make dough next morning, bake before lunchtime.

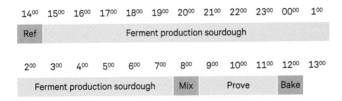

Notes

1. Production sourdough fermentation is about 17 hours. Can be shortened by refreshing starter in the evening rather than at lunchtime.

The examples above show how the long process of making sourdough rye bread can be timed to suit your life. Even these schedules are rather schematic and you should feel free to adjust them at will. The production sourdough is key here. It can easily ferment for anywhere from 12 to 24 hours. It gets progressively acidic as time goes on, boosting the sour flavour a bit and marginally inhibiting the yeasts. Once you feel confident with the idea, you can even try an eight-hour refreshment. Since the yeasts usually ferment more quickly than the lactic acid bacteria, you may find that such a young production sourdough will noticeably shorten proof time for the final dough. At the other extreme, a production sourdough that has sat around in your kitchen for 36 hours (for unavoidable reasons, naturally) may take quite a time to get going again. But when it does, the full flavour of the bread will be worth the wait.

Playing it cool

Wheat sourdoughs are not as forgiving as rye ones. Whereas in the latter a major build-up of acidity in the production sourdough is usually only good, it can have major negative effects on a wheat bread dough. The explanation for this apparent paradox is the nature of gluten. Rye gluten never forms that 'visco-elastic' structure that enables wheat dough to expand into a very light and aerated loaf. But an excess of acid compounds from an over-fermented sourdough will quickly tear a wheat dough to shreds.

So, when time-shifting wheat sourdoughs, we cannot arbitrarily decide that we will go from 4 hours to 12 hours just to suit ourselves. We need to control the speed at which the sourdough ferments and *temperature* is the best tool for this job.

The recipe for simple sourdough wheat bread in Chapter 3 took just over 11 hours from start to finish, with 4 hours for the Stage 2 production sourdough fermentation. That will fit within a day, of course, like this:

4. Afternoon delight

Refresh starter before lunch, make bread early evening, bake before bedtime.

1:00	2:00	3:00	4:00	5:00	6:00	7:00	8:00	9:00	10:00	11:00	12:00
											Ref

13:00	14:00	15:00	16:00	17:00	18:00	19:00	20:00	21:00	22:00	23:00	00:00
Ferment prod. sourdough				Mix	Prove					Bake	

Notes

1. This is a wheat sourdough schedule.
2. Production sourdough fermentation is 4 hours at room temperature.

But, with a four-hour refreshment and a five-hour final proof, there isn't a work- or sleep-sized slot in the schedule. We can create one by extending either the production sourdough refreshment or the final proof, or both.

If it is made with very cool water and kept in a cool place (not necessarily in the fridge) the production sourdough can be fermented over 12 or even 16 hours rather than 4. The final proof can also be retarded by making the dough cool and keeping the rising loaves cold.

Using these variables, the wheat sourdough bread becomes easily doable by people who are away from home all day. This is how it might work:

5. Commuter bake

Refresh starter before work, make bread early evening, bake (just) before bedtime.

1⁰⁰	2⁰⁰	3⁰⁰	4⁰⁰	5⁰⁰	6⁰⁰	7⁰⁰	8⁰⁰	9⁰⁰	10⁰⁰	11⁰⁰	12⁰⁰
						Ref	Ferment production sourdough				

13⁰⁰	14⁰⁰	15⁰⁰	16⁰⁰	17⁰⁰	18⁰⁰	19⁰⁰	20⁰⁰	21⁰⁰	22⁰⁰	23⁰⁰	00⁰⁰
Ferment production sourdough					Mix	Prove					Bake

Notes

1. This is a wheat sourdough schedule.
2. Production sourdough fermentation is about 10 hours in a cool place (10–12°C/50–54°F if possible). Make the final dough fairly warm (30°C/86°F) so that proof doesn't drag on into the small hours.

6. Overnight success

Refresh starter before work, make bread early evening, prove overnight and bake before breakfast.

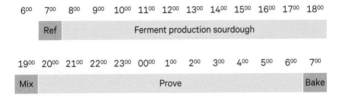

| 6⁰⁰ | 7⁰⁰ | 8⁰⁰ | 9⁰⁰ | 10⁰⁰ | 11⁰⁰ | 12⁰⁰ | 13⁰⁰ | 14⁰⁰ | 15⁰⁰ | 16⁰⁰ | 17⁰⁰ | 18⁰⁰ |

| | Ref | Ferment production sourdough | | | | | | | | | | |

| 19⁰⁰ | 20⁰⁰ | 21⁰⁰ | 22⁰⁰ | 23⁰⁰ | 00⁰⁰ | 1⁰⁰ | 2⁰⁰ | 3⁰⁰ | 4⁰⁰ | 5⁰⁰ | 6⁰⁰ | 7⁰⁰ |

| Mix | Prove | | | | | | | | | | | Bake |

Notes

1. This is a wheat sourdough schedule.
2. Production sourdough fermentation is about 11 hours in a cool place (10-12°C/50–54°F if possible).
3. Final proof is also about 11 hours. It may be necessary to prove the loaves in the fridge to stop them over-proving during the night. If so, give them 2 hours out of the fridge first to get the proof going. Loaves taken straight from the fridge will take a little longer to bake.
   Watch out for underbaked cores (the middle of the loaf). If in doubt, give it a little longer.

These examples show how time-shifting and changes of dough temperature can be used to work sourdough baking into everyday life. They are, however, no more than suggestions of what is possible and shouldn't necessarily be followed to the letter. Once you are familiar with which parts of the process allow some leeway and which don't, all fear of missed deadlines or spoiled loaves melts away. The most important thing to remember is to treat every dough on its merits. Whatever the recipe or the clock may say, only you can judge the right moment to take your dough to the next stage.

That's just the problem, you may be thinking. But the great thing about sourdough is that its slow tempo means that the 'right moment' is usually quite a long one. Laid-back baking, you might call it.

Wrap up

Baking our own bread brings the satisfaction of self-reliance, a sense of having some control over important things. Working with dough, a meeting place of physical coordination, sensory experience and mental serenity, is a pleasure both simple and profound.

If this book conveys one message, I hope it is this: making sourdough bread is do-able – no matter how crowded our life or how limited our previous experience. Once we have an idea of how microbes work, standing by while they turn flour and water into bread is a breeze.

With a simple starter and a grasp of the sourdough process, what better way to 'fill the unforgiving minute' than by nourishing ourselves with the best bread in the world?

Shaping soft sourdough rolls

Resources

Where next?

This book has demonstrated how easy it is to make sourdough, even if you don't seem to have time. But with sourdough, one thing leads to another in a very literal way. If you've got this far, you will probably be some way down the road that goes from intrigued to completely hooked.

So here are some signposts to further information, greater understanding and the wherewithal to make sourdough your natural partner for life.

READ books

These give reliable information on the microbiology of sourdough, the science of baking, the meaning of real bread, and the joys of fermentation and wood-fired baking.

Bread Matters, Andrew Whitley
(Fourth Estate, 2006)

The Bread Builders, Daniel Wing & Alan Scott
(Chelsea Green, 1999)

Bread Science, Emily Buehler
(Two Blue Books, 2006)

Bread, Jeffrey Hamelman
(Wiley, 2004)

Wild Fermentation, Sandor Ellix Katz
(Chelsea Green, 2003)

Build Your Own Earth Oven, Kiko Denzer
(sourdough recipes by Hannah Field)
(Hand Print Press, 3rd edition 2012)

JOIN the movement
The Real Bread Campaign
realbreadcampaign.org
The Grain Gathering (USA)
thegraingathering.com
Bread for Good Community Benefit Society (trading as Scotland
The Bread)
scotlandthebread.org

SEARCH for information
sustainweb.org/realbread/sourdough/
thefreshloaf.com
bbga.org (USA)
brockwell-bake.org.uk

LEARN to bake sourdough bread hands-on
bbga.org (USA)
e5bakehouse.com/classes (day courses in London)
schoolofartisanfood.org (short courses & one-year diploma)
sustainweb.org/realbread (a compendium of nearly a
hundred courses)
hobbshousebakery.co.uk (courses in Chipping Sodbury, nr Bristol)

FERMENT dry sourdough starters
breadmatters.com (my own original Russian rye starter)
sourdo.com (international starters from the USA)
breadtopia.com (USA)

EQUIP get basic kit
bakerybits.co.uk
breadmatters.com (proving baskets, couches, peels, blades, etc.)
breadtopia.com (USA)
kingarthurflour.com (USA)
souschef.co.uk

STOCK UP with organic flour
bobsredmill.com (USA)
dovesfarm.co.uk
fairhavenflour.com (USA)
gilchesters.com (rare breed grains stoneground on the farm in Northumberland)
kingarthurflour.com (USA)
marriagesmillers.co.uk
scotlandthebread.org (heritage and diverse wheat and rye flours)
shipton-mill.com
tcmg.org.uk (independent small watermills and windmills, often milling local heritage grains)

Oven temperature conversion chart

°C	°F	Gas	Description
135	275	1	Cool
150	300	2	
160	320	3	Warm
180	350	4	Moderate
190	375	5	
200	390	6	Fairly hot
210	410		
220	430	7	Hot
230	445	8	Very hot
240	465		
250	480	9	Very hot
260	500		

Andrew Whitley left a career as a producer in the BBC Russian Service in 1976 to found The Village Bakery, in Melmerby, Cumbria, which became one of the UK's leading organic bakeries.

For more than two decades he was the only commercial baker in the country using renewable energy by baking in wood-fired brick ovens. A visit in the early 1990s to post-communist Russia enabled him to study sourdough and he then launched a range of naturally fermented breads that met a sudden demand from people in the UK who found they could no longer tolerate factory loaves.

Andrew left The Village Bakery in 2002, did a Masters in Food Policy at City University and wrote *Bread Matters*, described by one reviewer as 'a searing critique of commercial baking methods'. *Bread Matters* won the André Simon 2006 Food Book Award.

In 2008, Andrew co-founded the Real Bread Campaign, which aims to bring good bread to every neighbourhood in the UK. In 2011, Andrew received the Special Judges' Award at the BBC Food & Farming Awards for 'changing the way we think about bread'. Until 2017 he and his late wife Veronica Burke ran popular courses for enthusiastic amateurs and community bakers at their agro-forestry smallholding near Edinburgh.

With Veronica, Andrew founded *Scotland The Bread*, a collaborative action research project to re-establish a Scottish flour and bread supply that is healthy, equitable, locally controlled and sustainable.

In 2018 *Scotland The Bread* installed a mill at the Bowhouse on the Balcaskie Estate in Fife where the project's diverse grains are grown. In 2019, Andrew moved to a new base near the Bowhouse where he continues to research locally resilient, nutritious and digestible bread-making grains – to make sourdough bread.

Index

Books in the series

Also available

Available in print, digital and audio formats from booksellers or via our website: **thedobook.co**

To hear about events and forthcoming titles, you can find us on social media **@dobookco**, or subscribe to our newsletter